高等院校应用型人才培养"十四五"规划旅游管理类系列教材

旅游英语应用文写作

主　编 ◎ 祁毕新月

Lǚyou Yingyu Yingyongwen Xiezuo

华中科技大学出版社
http://www.hustp.com
中国·武汉

图书在版编目(CIP)数据

旅游英语应用文写作/祁毕新月主编. —武汉:华中科技大学出版社,2021.9(2023.1 重印)
ISBN 978-7-5680-7325-7

Ⅰ.①旅… Ⅱ.①祁… Ⅲ.①旅游-英语-应用文-写作-职业教育-教材 Ⅳ.①F59

中国版本图书馆 CIP 数据核字(2021)第 189240 号

旅游英语应用文写作　　　　　　　　　　　　　　　　　　　　　　祁毕新月　主编
Lüyou Yingyu Yingyongwen Xiezuo

策划编辑：胡弘扬
责任编辑：陈　然
封面设计：原色设计
责任校对：李　弋
责任监印：周治超
出版发行：华中科技大学出版社(中国·武汉)　　电话：(027)81321913
　　　　　武汉市东湖新技术开发区华工科技园　　邮编：430223
录　　排：华中科技大学惠友文印中心
印　　刷：武汉科源印刷设计有限公司
开　　本：787mm×1092mm　1/16
印　　张：8.25　插页：2
字　　数：241 千字
版　　次：2023 年 1 月第 1 版第 2 次印刷
定　　价：35.80 元

本书若有印装质量问题，请向出版社营销中心调换
全国免费服务热线：400-6679-118　　竭诚为您服务
版权所有　侵权必究

出版说明

党的十九届五中全会确立了到2035年建成文化强国的远景目标,明确提出加快发展文化事业、文化产业和旅游业,推进文旅融合,实施创新发展,不断推动文化和旅游发展迈上新台阶。教育部于2019年和2021年先后颁布的《关于深化本科教育教学改革全面提高人才培养质量的意见》《本科层次职业教育专业设置管理办法(试行)》以及国务院于2019年颁布的《国家职业教育改革实施方案》,强调进一步推动高等教育应用型人才培养模式改革,对接产业需求,服务经济社会发展。

基于此,出版高水平的旅游管理类专业应用型人才培养教材,将助力旅游高等教育结构优化,促进旅游类应用型人才的能力培养与素质提升,进而为中国旅游业在"十四五"期间深化文旅融合、持续迈向高质量发展提供有力支撑。

华中科技大学出版社一向以服务高校教学、科研为己任,重视高品质专业教材出版,"十三五"期间,在教育部高等学校旅游管理类专业教学指导委员会和全国高校旅游应用型本科院校联盟的大力支持和指导下,在全国范围内特邀国家"万人计划"教学名师、近百所应用型院校旅游管理专业学科带头人、一线骨干"双师双能型"教师,以及旅游行业精英等担任顾问和编者,组织编纂出版"高等院校应用型人才培养'十三五'规划旅游管理类系列教材"。该套系教材自出版发行以来,被全国近百所开设旅游管理类专业的院校选用,并多次再版。

为积极响应"十四五"期间我国文旅行业发展及旅游高等教育发展的新趋势,"高等院校应用型人才培养'十四五'规划旅游管理类系列教材"项目应运而生。本项目依据文旅行业的最新发展和学术研究的最新进展,立足旅游管理应用型人才培养特征进行整体规划,将高水平的"十三五"规划教材修订、丰富、再版,同时开发出一批教学紧缺、业态急需的教材。本项目在以下三个方面做出了创新。

一是紧扣旅游学科特色,创新教材编写理念。本套教材基于旅游高等教育发展新形势,结合新版旅游管理专业人才培养方案,遵循应用型人才培养的内在逻辑,在编写团队、编写内容与编写体例上充分彰显旅游管理应用型专业的学科优势,全面提升旅游管理专业学生的实践能力与创新能力。

二是遵循理论与实践并重原则,构建多元化知识结构。在产教融合思想的指导下,坚持以案例为引领,同步案例与知识链接贯穿全书,增设学习目标、实训项目、本章小结、关键概念、案例解析、实训操练和相关链接等个性化模块。

三是依托资源服务平台,打造新形态立体教材。华中科技大学出版社紧抓"互联网+"时代教育需求,自主研发并上线了华中出版资源服务平台,为本套系教材提供立体化教学配套服务,

既为教师教学提供便捷,提供教学计划书、教学课件、习题库、案例库、参考答案、教学视频等系列配套教学资源,又为教学管理提供便捷,构建集课程开发、习题管理、学生评论、班级管理等于一体的教学生态链,真正打造出线上线下、课堂课外的新形态立体化互动教材。

本项目编委会力求通过出版一套兼具理论与实践、传承与创新、基础与前沿的精品教材,为我国加快实现旅游高等教育内涵式发展、建成世界旅游强国贡献一份力量,并诚挚邀请更多致力于中国旅游高等教育的专家学者加入我们!

华中科技大学出版社

Preface 前 言

近年来,我国旅游业迅猛发展,成为国民经济的重要增长点。随着国内外旅游业务的不断扩大,旅游英语应用文在旅游相关的工作和生活中,发挥着不可替代的重要作用。为了适应旅游职业教育发展的需要,根据国家教育部制定的旅游类专业教学计划和教学大纲的要求,我们编写了《旅游英语应用文写作》一书。

旅游应用文是服务于旅游活动的一种应用文体。在长期的使用过程中,旅游应用文逐渐形成了与其他应用文体不同的特点,成为一门独立的应用性学科。旅游应用文是用来解决旅游工作和生活中的实际问题的,具有很强的实用性、针对性和时效性,同时在写作上又很讲究规范性,必须遵循一定的格式及内容要求。

本书共分为八章,涵盖了旅游目的地宣传、旅游招贴和通知、旅游商务信函、旅游日程安排、旅游常用表格、求职简历、旅游合同和旅游广告。

本书在内容编排上,主要突出以下特色。一是所选内容有代表性和实用性,适合课堂教学和学生操练。旅游应用文种类繁多,而旅游院校应用文写作课程课时有限,所以要求教材所选内容必须具有代表性,且对学生将来从事旅游方面的工作要有实际指导意义。笔者在选材时充分考虑了这一要求。二是每章所选的应用文实例来源广泛、文体多样,力求内容新,语言规范、地道,实用价值高。三是突出旅游应用文不同文体的常用词汇、搭配及句式,配以精心设计的习题,便于学生切实提高应用文写作能力。四是将旅游应用文的教学与英语基础写作结合起来,特别在本书最后一章强调了英语写作基本功的重要性及培养方法。

在编写过程中,笔者参考了国内外大量的资料,在此一并向有关作者表示衷心的感谢。限于编者水平,书中定有疏漏谬误之处,敬请读者指正。

Contents

Page	
1	Chapter 1 Promotion of Tourist Destinations
23	Chapter 2 Tourism Posters and Notices
34	Chapter 3 Letter Writing
50	Chapter 4 Itineraries
68	Chapter 5 Application Forms in Tourism Industry
85	Chapter 6 CVs and Cover Letters
100	Chapter 7 Contracts in Tourism Industry
112	Chapter 8 Advertisements in Tourism Industry
124	Bibliography

Chapter 1

Promotion of Tourist Destinations

Ⅰ. Introductions

Promotion of tourist destinations refers to a series of information transmission and communication activities to expand the source of tourists, and to increase tourism consumption for certain tourist destinations. The purpose of tourism publicity is to promote tourism products. Tourism product is a special kind of commodity, since the natural scenery, historical relics and local customs of tourist destinations cannot be carried away, moved or displayed. When tourists do not know about them, they will not buy it easily. Therefore, the promotion of tourist destinations is crucial.

Tourism publicity on one hand, plays the role of information transmission, informing potential tourists of stories or news related to tourist destinations and enhancing their market visibility; on the other hand, by establishing the beautiful image of tourist products, tourism publicity can arouse the consumption desire of the potential tourists.

The following points need to be taken into account when preparing a destination promotion:

1. Practical. The information provided in tourism publicity materials should be true, comprehensive and up-to-date.

2. Appealing. Tourism publicity should be beautifully worded to stimulate the enthusiasm of travel in target tourists.

3. Scientific. The intrinsic logic of content cannot be ignored.

Ⅱ. Sample Reading

Sample 1　National-level tourist destinations

Travel in China—A Brief Introduction to China

Situated in eastern Asia, and on the western shore of the Pacific Ocean, the People's Republic of China covers a land area of around 9.6 million square kilometers, with an inland and coastal water area of more than 4.7 million square kilometers, and an eastern and southern continental coastline extending for about 18000 kilometers. Its vast maritime territory is studded with 7600 islands, of which Taiwan is the largest with an area of 35798 square kilometers. China shares common borders with 14 countries and is adjacent to 8 nations on the ocean. There are 4 municipalities directly under central government administration, 23 provinces, 5 autonomous regions and 2 special administrative regions. The capital city of China is Beijing.

Name: The People's Republic of China, commonly known as China

Capital: Beijing

Population: about 1.4 billion (2021)

Land Area: Approximately 9.6 million square kilometers

Geographic Location: In eastern Asia and on the western shore of the Pacific Ocean

National Flag: On September 27, 1949, the First Plenary Session of the Chinese People's Political Consultative Conference adopted a resolution establishing the national flag of the People's Republic of China as a red flag with five stars. The flag is red in color, which symbolizes revolution, and rectangular in shape with the proportion between the length and height being 3 to 2. The five five-pointed yellow stars are located in the upper left corner, one of them, which is the largest, appears on the left, while the other four hem it on the right. This represents the great unity of the Chinese people under the leadership of the Communist Party of China (CPC).

National Anthem: On September 27, 1949, the First Plenary Session of the Chinese People's Political Consultative Conference adopted the resolution that the national anthem of the People's Republic of China be "March of the Volunteers".

National Emblem: On June 23, 1950, the second session of the First Plenary Session of the Chinese People's Political Consultative Conference adopted the design for the national emblem of the People's Republic of China. The National Emblem of the People's Republic of China, "shall comprise the design of Tian'anmen in its centre illuminated by five stars and encircled by ears of grain and a cogwheel, which symbolizes the New Democratic Revolution of China since the May 4 Movement (1919) and the birth of the People's Republic of China under the people's democratic dictatorship led by the working class and based on the alliance of workers and peasants".

Ethnic Groups: There are 56 ethnic groups in China, among which the Han people account for 92% of the total population while the other 55 ethnic groups account for 8%.

Languages and characters: Chinese is the common language, and Chinese characters are the common scripts. Fifty-three ethnic groups speak their own distinct languages and 23 ethnic groups have their own writing scripts.

Religions: Religions represented in China include Buddhism, Daoism, Islam, Catholicism and other Christian groups. People are free to pursue any religion.

Major Holidays: National Day—October 1; International Labor Day—May 1; New Year's Day—January 1; Spring Festival—first day of the lunar calendar—this is the biggest festival in China.

Currency: RMB ¥

Time Difference: 8 hours earlier than GMT

Climate: Eastern Asia monsoon climate

Natural Profile: The People's Republic of China, with a land area of around 9.6 million square kilometers and a water area of about 4.73 million square kilometers, is the biggest country in Asia and the third largest country in the world. The topography descends toward sea level from west to east and gives rise to a variety of landform. Mount Everest in the Himalayan mountain ranges and lying on the southeast edge of China at 8848 meters above sea level, is the world's highest peak. The Yangtze River and Yellow River, 6300 kilometers and 5464 kilometers long respectively, are the most important rivers in China. And the Jinghang Canal, which stretches for 1794 kilometers, is one of the longest artificial canals in the world. Qinghai Lake has an area of 4583 square kilometers and is the largest inland salt water lake in China while Poyang Lake with an area of 3583 square kilometers is China's largest freshwater lake. China experiences a complex and varied climate. Most parts of the country lie in the northern temperate zone and subtropical zone and belong to the eastern Asia monsoon climatic area. In winter, the climate is cold and dry and the temperature difference between the South and the North can be forty degrees centigrade, while in summer temperatures are high, it is the rainy season and temperature differences are small. However, precipitation varies from 1500 mm in the southeast to less than 50 mm in the northwest. The extremely high mountainous regions have constantly cold weather and the Qinghai-Tibet Plateau has a unique plateau climate, with a variety of mineral elements and abundant water resources.

History: China, with a recorded history of more than 5000 years, is one of the four ancient civilizations. From the time of the founding of Xia Dynasty in the 21st century BC to the late Spring and Autumn period, with the Shang and Western Zhou Dynasties in between, society was slavery based. From the time of the Warring States period of 475 BC to the early period of the Qing Dynasty, with Qin, Western Han, Eastern Han, Three Kingdom, Western Jin, Eastern Jin, Southern and Northern Dynasties, Sui, Tang, Five Dynasties, Song, Yuan, and Ming Dynasties in between, society was feudal. After the Opium War in 1840, China gradually turned into a semi-colonial and semi-feudal society, as a result of imperialist invasion. In 1911, the 1911 Revolution, led by Sun Yat-sen, ended the monarchy and on October 1, 1949, the CPC, under the leadership of Mao Zedong, led the Chinese people and established the People's Republic of China.

Economy: China has a relatively mature industrial system, with established commercial categories and products. Agriculture holds an important place in the economy and the output of grains, cotton, sugar, oil, tea and other agricultural products is among the highest in the world. China's handcrafts industry is also world famous for its sophistication and skill. China has now built a traffic and transport network with railways, highways, waterways and airlines as the main contributors to this infrastructure.

Singapore: at a glance

If God does exist, he probably lives in the clouds above Singapore. Travelers who have witnessed it refer to this tiny city—sheltered by the Southern extremity of the Malay Peninsula—as the Garden of Eden, one of the most fantastic and magnetic places in the world. It charms guests with a most peculiar combination of ancient traditions, in perfect fusion with the latest achievements in science and technology, primeval nature and futuristic buildings. Today, this vivid and multi-faceted Singapore, while still one of the top 20 smallest countries in the world, is an incredibly compelling magnet for

tourists from all over the world and inexhaustible source of captivating discoveries and entertainment.

The name Singapore stands for an island, a state and a city at the same time and it represents one of the most amazing and paradoxical places in the world. It has managed to develop itself from an arid, infertile island with no natural resources into a highly developed Asian megalopolis in a century and a half, and now ranks well into the list of the world's richest cities. The sheer number of varied sights that are concentrated in Singapore is totally disproportionate to its tiny area of land, yet the uniqueness of these sights stokes the fires of rapid growth in this wonder-island's touristic popularity. It is the only place, where guests can admire a city from the largest Ferris wheel in the world, swim in an outdoor swimming pool at the height of 200 meters, before walking along a double helix-shaped bridge and testing their stamina on the most breathtaking of theme park rides.

Singapore charms every single visitor with its ultramodern buildings, whose inconceivable shapes evoke emotions from fantastic movies. Skyscrapers standing in an orderly manner, while striking the eye with their peculiar shapes, are harmonically combined with the florid labyrinths of the ancient Chinatown's buildings; this is a combination of cosmic high-tech constructions and elegant buildings from colonial times.

Even more fascinating is the opportunity to stroll through a genuine tropical forest, where the amusing macaques rock on the treetops and hundreds of exotic birds fill the air with their songs, people can enjoy all this without leaving the city. Unique landscape parks and nature reserves with tropical inhabitants are among Singapore's most valuable treasures and are fiercely protected by locals.

This micro-state has many vivid characters. Singapore's downtown is as motley as league of nations living here, citizens of various nationalities with different cultural codes and religions help create the inimitable aura of this tiny country. It is one of the places in the world, where one can get acquainted with traditions of several disparate cultures in a single day; and only here, people can exit the mosque, cross the street and enter a Hindu temple or pagoda.

In addition to its historical culture, Singapore is an ideal spot for gastro-tourism. Countless local restaurants, cafes and catering centers offer a palette of unique flavors and aromas, enough to make you feel giddy. Singapore's culinary offerings are amazingly rich: authentic Chinese, Indian, Thai, Malayan and Japanese dishes are all readily at the tourists' disposal.

This Asian megalopolis is also famous as one of the cleanest and well-attended cities in the world. The locals' aspiration for order is absolute and they meticulously keep the streets spotless. Residents also take care of their own and tourists' comfort. Almost all tourist zones and important city routes are protected from the scorching tropical sun with huge umbrellas; while there are virtually each indoor places have air-conditioner, this is useful for a country with an average annual temperature of 26～30℃.

Singapore is a dynamic city that lives at the tempo of a never ending holiday. A plethora of free performances are organized across the country every evening, including laser shows and music fans' shows, concerts and theatre performances.

This amazing city develops in rapid pace and creates new unique projects every year. Thus, no matter how often you visit Singapore, it will provide you surprise and delight, and offer more opportunities for vivid and eventful holiday and for unforgettable impressions.

Sample 2　A provincial-level tourist destination

Tibet is a land rich in culture heritage. Situated on the Qinghai-Tibetan plateau, the land has the world's highest mountains, several large, rushing rivers and many beautiful lakes. While the northern part is on a high plateau and is a wildlife reserve (Changtang National Nature Reserve, 300000 km^2), the southern, eastern, and western

parts are valleys. Its unique culture, celebrated monasteries and its magnificent scenery make it charming and mysterious. The mountains, including Mount Everest, are imposing with their snow-covered heights.

Tibet Travel Documents

Besides a valid passport and a valid Chinese visa, you need two different kinds of permits for traveling in Tibet: the entry permit (TTB permit) and the Aliens' Travel Document (if you want to visit the unopened area in Tibet).

Best Time to Go

It is suitable for travel to Tibet from April to early November, and the best time is August and September. But if you only stay in Lhasa, you can go there at any time of the year. It is important to get the real time weather report.

Scenic Spots and Places of Historic Interest in Tibet

Most popular scenic spots in Tibet are Lhasa, Zedang, Shigatse, Dingri, Dangxiong. Mount Qomolangma (or Mount Everest) and Holy Mountain are hit places for exploration and excursions because they are always full of mystery and excitement.

What to Pack

High altitude medications, sunscreen, sunglasses, lip creams and roper clothing.

High Altitude Travel Tips

Avoid catching a cold before entering Tibet; take a good rest, drink more water, and do not take shower at the first day; avoid alcohol and do not smoke; take things a little bit slowly.

Tibet Travel Taboos

Do not take pictures without permission; do not talk about sensitive issues like politics and religion; never touch Tibetan people on the head. Be aware of Tibetan customs and taboos.

Sample 3　A municipal-level tourist destination

Suzhou, A prosperous and classic city in China

Suzhou is the most exquisite garden city in China, noted for its unique layout, intertwined with waterways, stone bridges and private gardens.

Classic Suzhou Overview

Suzhou, a city of eastern China, is only one-hour drive from Shanghai, on the lower reaches of the Yangtze River and on the shores of Lake Taihu in the Province of Jiangsu. It was the capital (6th-5th century BC) of an ancient vassal state—the Wu Kingdom of the Zhou Dynasty. It was renamed Suzhou in the 6th century AD and is famous for its classical gardens, beautiful stone bridges, pagodas, silk, Grand Canal and canal-side housing, which have contributed to its status as one of the great tourist attractions.

Since ancient times, Suzhou has always been one of the most prosperous cities in China. The GDP per capita was RMB 179200 ($26000) in 2019, ranked the fourth place among 659 Chinese cities.

Location and Population

Suzhou lies in the Yangtze Delta, bordering Shanghai in the east, Zhejiang Province in the south, Lake Taihu in the west and the Yangtze River in the north. Its east longitude is between 119°55′ E and 121°20′ E and its north latitude is between 30°47′ N and 32°02′ N with an average altitude of about 4 meters. The total area of Suzhou is 8657.32 km^2, 2.7% of that mountainous, 42.5% under water. The land under cultivation occupies 288160 hectares. Built-up urban areas cover 1650 km^2.

Suzhou is composed of Suzhou Downtown and 4 county-level cities. Suzhou Downtown contains six Districts: Wuzhong, Xiangcheng, Gusu, Wujiang, Suzhou Industrial Park and Suzhou New Hi-tech District. The 4 county-level cities are Changshu, Kunshan, Taicang and Zhangjiagang.

Suzhou has a population of 7.44 million (2020).

History and Culture

Suzhou, the cradle of Wu culture, is one of the oldest towns in the Yangtze River Delta region, which retains much of its original character. 2500 years ago in the late Shang Dynasty, local tribes who named themselves "Gou Wu" lived in the area which in time would become the modern city of Suzhou. After the completion of the Beijing-Hangzhou Grand Canal, the city began to thrive. Suzhou served as the centre of silk trade along the bustling waterway. Marco Polo once marveled at the city's prosperity and he recorded that its inhabitants were comprised of "prudent merchants, and, as already observed, skillful in all the arts". Polo noted that a number of the Suzhou people were learned in natural science, were good physicians and able philosophers. In Polo's words, the city of Suzhou was "great" and "noble".

During the Ming Dynasty (1368-1644), with an increased concentration of silk manufacturers, Suzhou became a leading silk fashion center.

However, the city also faced difficult times, during the 1860's, Suzhou was occupied during the end of the Taiping Rebellion and then again in World War Ⅱ.

With the foundation of the People's Republic of China in 1949, Suzhou has once again rightly reclaimed its fame and developed into one of the most prosperous cities in

China. As far as tourism development is concerned, it has been chosen as one of China's 24 historical and cultural cities and is one of four tourist cities with top environmental protection (the other three being Beijing, Hangzhou and Guilin). In 1997, Suzhou caught the world's attention by having its classic gardens inscribed on the UNESCO list as a World Cultural Heritage Site. Since then, tourism has grown along with a burgeoning economy.

Economy

Suzhou is the largest economy in Jiangsu Province, which has been recognized as the "Most Aspiring City of Prosperity and Civilization in the Southeast of China". In the 1970s and 1980s, Suzhou's economy developed with the growth of township enterprises and collective enterprises, but during the 1990s, Suzhou adjusted its development strategy, leveraging on its state level development zones to attract a large amount of foreign investment and energized the development of an externally oriented economy.

City Infrastructure

Being an important economic and tourist city, Suzhou has made great improvement to its infrastructures. It is accessible by train, bus, boat and plane.

The railway, Jinghu Railway (Nanjing-Shanghai), passes through the city and Suzhou Railway Station is among the busiest passenger stations in China, having 139 trains stopping daily.

Suzhou is also conveniently linked by several highway/expressway including Huning (Shanghai-Nanjing) Expressway, and Suzhou-Hangzhou Expressway. The new Suzhou Outer Ring Expressway was completed in 2005, connecting the peripheral county-level cities of Taicang, Kunshan, and Changshu. Sutong Yangtze River Bridge opened in June 2008, connecting Nantong and Changshu of Suzhou jurisdiction and making it a new transportation hub for communication between the north and south of

Jiangsu.

Suzhou is abundant in water resources, including many canals, rivers and lakes. The waterway is one of the most convenient transportations for locals, travelers and cargo. Taking these rivers and canals, you can easily reach its water towns, neighboring cities including Hangzhou, the capital city of Zhejiang Province, and Suzhou Port.

Suzhou has its own airport, named Suzhou Guangfu Airport, but this airport is principally a military base and is only partially used for civic transportation. Three nearby airports, Wuxi Shuofang Airport, Shanghai Hongqiao International Airport and Pudong International Airport, serve visitors to the city.

Sample 4   Scenic spots

Tiger Hill

This hill sits 3.5 kilometers to the northwest of the downtown area and has the reputation of being the most beautiful scenic spot in Jiangsu Province. Su Dongpo, a famous Song Dynasty poet, spoke fondly of Tiger Hill, saying, "It's a pity not to visit Tiger Hill when travelling in Suzhou."

Tiger Hill is an attractive, meaningful tourist destination and as far back as the late Spring and Autumn Period (770-476 BC), Fu Chai, the King of Wu, buried his father on the hill. Three days after the funeral was held, a white tiger was spotted at the top of the hill, hence the name.

The brothers Wang Xun and Wang Min, senior officials during Eastern Jin Dynasty (317-420 AD), built villas on the hill, then donated the residences to be used as Tiger Hill Temple. During the Tang Dynasty, in order to not conflict with the title of Emperor Taizu, the temple was renamed Wuqiu Bao'en Temple.

In 825-826, Bai Juyi, the famous Tang Dynasty poet serving as the governor of

Suzhou, asked the people to dig a canal at the hill foot and to build a dam on it, which was known as Baidi (now Shantang Street). The work was done so that water would run around the hill to provide a quiet, secluded, scenic spot.

During the reign of the Emperor Taizong of the early Song Dynasty (995-997), the temple was rebuilt and renamed the Yunyan Temple. It was listed as one of the 10 most important Buddhist Temples on the five famous mountains during the Song Dynasty, and it is a magnificent sight, with pagodas and pavilions tucked away among the trees. From the Song Dynasty to the Qing Dynasty, the temple was badly damaged several times, but the remaining architecture was refurbished during the Tongzhi and Guangxu periods of the Qing Dynasty (1862-1908), with the exception of the Yunyan Tower and Second Mountain Gate.

The Tiger Hill gives an impression of serenity with its pagoda and temple. The 1000-year-old Yunyan Temple and pagoda appear plain, yet they are remarkable structures.

Broken-Beam Hall, from the Yuan Dynasty, is a fantastic structure in its own right.

There are many other scenic spots with legendary fame, such as "Sword Pond" on the precipice; "Flying-girder Gully", a cliff pavilion; Hanhan Spring to the front of the hill; "Try-the-sword Rock"; Zhenniang Tomb; "Thousand-men Rock", "Two Immortals Pavilion", "White Lotus Pond", "Nodding Rock", "Two Hanging Buckets".

Tourists can visit the older part of Suzhou and enjoy the scenes of the surrounding countryside by visiting Xiaowu Pavilion, Wangsu, or the Zhishuang Pavilion on top of the hill.

Ticket prices: 40 yuan/person, off-season; 60 yuan/person, peak season

Peak season: Apr 16-Oct 30; off-season: Oct 31-Apr 15

Address: No. 8 Huqiu Mountain Gate

Getting there: Tiger Hill is about 3 km from the Suzhou Railway Station. Take

tourist bus No. 1, No. 2, No. 8, No. 32, No. 146, or No. 949.

Ride through the Great Smoky Mountains during Peak Fall Foliage with This Railroad Experience

All aboard for an incredible fall foliage viewing experience!

Nothing says autumn quite like admiring the red, yellow, and orange hues of the changing leaves. And this November, fall foliage fanatics can embark on a special train journey through the Great Smoky Mountains with prime views of the colorful trees.

The Watauga Valley Railroad Historical Society and Museum has organized an event on November 1. This event will take guests along the Great Smoky Mountains Railroad through the mountains and picturesque countryside of North Carolina. The excursion will start in Bryson City, North Carolina, before making its way to Nantahala Gorge and then back to Bryson.

The trip covers most of the current operating trackage of the Great Smoky Mountains Railroad. The route hugs the banks of the Little Tennessee and Nantahala rivers, and crosses Fontana Lake on a trestle standing 100 feet above the water. All the while, guests can look out their windows to take in the view.

But this full-day rail excursion actually begins before the train leaves the station, as ticket holders can enjoy complimentary admission to the Smoky Mountain Trains Museum, which boasts a collection of 7000 Lionel engines, cars and accessories, a children's activity center, and more.

For their onboard experience, passengers can choose between Crown, Tourist Coach, or Open-air Coach tickets (First-class tickets have already sold out). All classes offer seating in vintage, restored passenger cars with heating (except Open-air Coach). Tourist Coach cars feature ceiling fans and windows that open and close for fresh-air viewing, while Crown cars offer larger windows for better viewing, although these do not open. First-class passengers will be treated to lounge car seating and stunning views through large windows that also do not open. The first-class ticket also includes meals and dessert. Passengers in other classes may order a boxed lunch as they purchase their ticket, or bring their own food.

Ticket prices range from $70 to $159 per person. For more information, visit the official website of the Watauga Valley Railroad Historical Society & Museum.

Lindt Opens World's Largest Chocolate Museum— With the World's Largest Chocolate Fountain

If you ever watched the movie "Charlie and the Chocolate Factory", lamenting that such a magical place did not exist, get ready for a pleasant surprise. On September 13, 2020, the Lindt Home of Chocolate will open in Zurich, and while it may not have everlasting gobstoppers, it's still pure paradise for anyone with a sweet tooth.

The Lindt Home of Chocolate takes guests on a journey with an interactive museum bringing them through "seven chocolate worlds". From cultivation to production, the cocoa bean that gifts the world with chocolate is the star of the story. The exhibits will also teach visitors about the history of Swiss chocolate making, teaching them not only about Lindt, but also about its famous predecessors.

The Home of Chocolate also features several other attractions to keep chocolate lovers busy. At the Lindt Chocolateria, for example, guests can create their own tasty confections during a chocolate-making class, while the research facility allows an inside look at the Lindt production process. The Praline Tasting Room is also a must, and a Lindt cafe is available to cleanse the palate and refuel for more exploring.

Unlike Willy Wonka's factory, guests here are encouraged to take candy home, and it's easy, considering that the building also houses the world's largest Lindt chocolate shop. While the maze of white, milk, and dark chocolates is impressive, the Lindt Home of Chocolate also boasts another record: the world's largest chocolate fountain. Standing at about 30 feet tall, this show-stopping fountain beats out the previous record holder by just a few feet. It's also the centerpiece greeting guests at the entrance, setting the tone for the chocolaty experience ahead.

The Lindt & Sprüngli factory has sat in Kilchberg, Zurich since 1899. The Lindt Home of Chocolate—a project seven years in the making—was designed to perfectly complement that historic building and serve as a beacon to chocolate lovers everywhere.

Lounge Review: British Airways Galleries Club Lounge (North), Heathrow Terminal 5

Background

London Heathrow Airport has four terminals (Terminals 2 to 5), with British Airways (BA) operating mostly from Terminal 5.

Galleries Club Lounges here are located at the North and South wings, in Terminal 5A (Galleries Club lounges correspond to business class lounges).

Where is it?

Immediately after the security check-in Terminal 5A.

Who can access it?

Customers travelling in British Airways' First Class, Club World or Club Europe, Executive Club Gold and Silver Members (plus one guest), one world Emerald and Sapphire members (plus one guest) can access this lounge.

What's it like?

The British Airways logo at the entrance is unmissable, signalling you from afar.

Being welcomed by the smiling face of the staff is never a bad thing, especially when it is before an early morning long-haul trip.

My boarding pass is scanned and I walk in; on my right are newspapers and magazines and on the left are food counters (tea, coffee, crisps, cookies, wine and water).

The lounge is very large with ample seating areas featuring Osborne and Little-designed fabric. It is well lit with ample natural light flowing in through the large windows adjoining the tarmac. A few shower rooms are dedicated to passengers wanting to fresh up before their flights. There are large community tables, however, I head towards the high tables adjoining the window and facing the tarmac, where I take a seat. There are also lounge chairs around, but I choose the high tables as they offer more privacy.

I enjoy a cup of coffee with cookies as I look at some of the aircraft taxiing around in front of me—an aviation geek's paradise.

Charging points are easily found where I plug in my phone and marking my space, I also check out the breakfast area.

Food and drink

A wide selection of hot and cold food is quite appealing, but I decided to opt for a light meal since I plan to eat on the plane as well.

There is a hot food area with pasta, baked beans, rice and curry; while the salad counter has a range of fresh vegetables and leaves with a few dressings.

There is a wide choice of bread and pastries, cold cuts and other breakfast items that make up my plate.

Verdict: Easy to find and access. Highly recommended for passengers wanting some quiet time in a luxurious space before their flight. Equipped with conveniences and a wide-array of food options.

Hours: 5:30 to 22:30

Location: Terminal 5A, London Heathrow Airport

Ⅲ. Useful Words and Expressions

coastline n. 海岸线

autonomous region 自治区

special administrative region 特别行政区

geographic location 地理位置

national flag 国旗

national anthem 国歌

national emblem 国徽

ethnic group 民族

sea level 海平面

heritage n. 遗产

plateau n. 高原

unique adj. 独特的,独一无二的

wildlife reserve 野生动物保护区

taboo n. 禁忌,忌讳

legacy n. 遗产,遗留

landscape n. 风景,景色

appreciate v. 欣赏

architecture group 建筑群

altitude n. 高度,海拔

sightseeing tunnel 观光隧道

Ⅳ. Sentence Examples

1. Situated in eastern Asia, and on the western shore of the Pacific Ocean, the People's Republic of China covers a land area of about 9.6 million km^2...

中国位于亚洲大陆的东部、太平洋西岸,陆地面积约 960 万平方千米。

2. The Beijing-Hangzhou Grand Canal, which stretches for 1794 km, is one of the longest artificial canals in the world.

绵延 1794 千米的京杭大运河是世界上最长的运河之一。

3. China, with a recorded history of more than 5000 years, is one of the four ancient civilizations.

中国拥有五千多年的历史,是四大文明古国之一。

4. Most parts of the country lie in the northern temperate zone.

我国大部分地区位于北温带。

5. Agriculture holds an important place in the economy.

农业在我国经济中占有重要地位。

6. It is suitable for travel to Tibet from April to early November, and the best time is August and September.

从四月到十一月初适宜到西藏旅游,其中八九月是最佳时间。

7. Tibet is a land rich in culture heritage.

西藏有着丰富的文化遗产。

8. Its unique culture, celebrated monasteries and its magnificent scenery make it charming and mysterious.

独特的文化、享有盛誉的寺院和壮丽的自然风光使西藏充满了神秘和魅力。

9. Mount Qomolangma and Holy Mountain are hit places for exploration and excursions because they are always full of mystery.

珠穆朗玛峰和神山总是那么神秘莫测,因而是探险和徒步的热门地点。

10. The 6-square-kilometer West Lake is the pride of Hangzhou.

西湖面积为 6 平方公里,它是杭州市的骄傲。

11. Scholars and poets have left a legacy of rhapsodic poetry and prose after visits to the lake.

无数的诗人和学者在游览西湖后留下了动人心魄的诗篇和美文。

12. As a landmark of Shanghai, the Bund is a must for visitors who come to Shanghai.

外滩作为上海的标志,是旅游者们的必到之处。

Ⅴ. Notes

1. a semi-colonial and semi-feudal society 半殖民地半封建社会

2. the Himalayan mountain range 喜马拉雅山脉

3. Mount Everest or Mount Qomolangma 珠穆朗玛峰

4. Zedang，Shigatse，Dingri，Dangxiong 均为西藏地名，分别指泽当、日喀则、定日和当雄

5. Holy Mountain 西藏神山

Ⅵ. Practice

1. Translation.

①黄山位于中国安徽省南部。

②长江三峡壮丽的自然美，使无数诗人和画家为之陶醉，留下了不可胜数的诗篇和美文。

③The people of Hangzhou regard the West Lake as an important facet of their daily life.

④The West Lake is definitely a place worth going to.

2. Please complete the following tourism promotion with appropriate words or phrases.

"East or west, Guilin landscape is best!" _____ （位于）in the northeast of Guangxi Zhuang Autonomous Region in south China, Guilin is considered to be the pearl of China's thriving tourist industry on account of the natural beauty and historic treasures. _____ （拥有）an area of about 27800 square kilometers, the city is rather compact when compared with other major _____ _____ （旅游城市）in the country. The stunning _____ （风景）in which the city is situated has a kind of magic that is all its own. The strangely shaped hills or karsts, with the verdant vegetation ranging from bamboos to conifers together with _____

_____ (清澈见底的) waters and wonderful caves make Guilin such an appealing destination. Guilin is also an important cultural city with a history of more than 2000 years. The city has been the political, economic and cultural center of Guangxi since the Northern Song Dynasty (960-1127).

3. Write a promotion material for Yuyuan Garden according to the following directions.

景区分类:主题公园

开放时间:9:00—16:30

门票价格:40元

联系方式:021-63260830

地址:上海市黄浦区福佑路168号

投诉电话:021-64393615

概述:豫园是上海市区唯一留存完好的江南古典园林,全国重点文物保护单位。豫园始建于明嘉靖三十八年(1559年),后经多次修葺,古园更臻完美,为游乐观瞻极佳去处。现占地30余亩,全园擅江南园林之胜,有萃秀堂、仰山堂、三穗堂、玉华堂、点春堂、万花楼、会景楼、快楼、鱼乐榭、大假山等40多处胜景。

Chapter 2

Tourism Posters and Notices

Ⅰ. Introductions

Tourism posters mainly include notices to tourists from tourist attractions, notices in daily work of travel agencies, exhibitions and conferences, and other posters.

When writing notices in English, please pay attention to the following aspects:

1. Before the main text, write the title, which is usually Notice or the name of the meeting;

2. The content of the main text includes the reason, time, place, informant, etc.

Ⅱ. Sample Reading

Sample 1   Notice of a meeting

Notice

The meeting will be held in the conference room of the hotel at 10:00 a.m. on

February 12,2010. All managers are invited to attend.

Holliday Inn

Feb. 9, 2010

Sample 2 Notice of an exhibition

The 10th Hangzhou West Lake Expo

Time: October 18-November 8

Address: Hangzhou, Zhejiang Province

Contents: The West Lake Expo has a total number of 102 exhibition activities, including the most influential and powerful players in the Chinese tourism sector. At the same time, it focuses on the introduction of new projects. 40 new projects are in evidence, such as the International Sister Cities' Mayors Summit, The General Assembly for Global Finance, the International Tourism Festival of the West Lake Expo, the First Suitable Living Festival, the First Leisure and Shopping Festival of Hangzhou and the Performance Entertainment Expo, etc. The 10th Hangzhou West Lake Expo broke with tradition and established a new Expo form—"West Lake Expo on the Internet". The 10th Hangzhou West Lake Expo combined both Internet and "real" exhibitions to highlight the features of "enjoyment and experience". This Expo has been divided into 5 categories to highlight "The past, the present and the future".

Sample 3　Notice of a conference

International Conference for Reviving Tourism and Dealing with Crisis

Time: November 16-18

Address: Hangzhou, Zhejiang Province

Contents: The aim of this conference is to gain support from the international tourism industry, and restore the confidence of international markets in tourism in Sichuan after the earthquake. The conference will focus on how the tourism industry can deal with the adverse effects of sudden crisis, and share successful experiences of effective communication and forward planning, as well as tourism restoration. A discussion platform will be set up to deal with development, changes and trends in global tourism market.

Sample 4　Notice of an event

Events Information on Polish National Day

Let's Dance Chopin

When: May 22, 5:00 p.m.

Where: Expo, Auditorium Expo Center

Have you ever danced Chopin? Worldwide premiere of a Chopin's music-inspired dance show involving 100 artists from all over the world, dancing to the music performed by the Polish Orchestra "Simfonia Iuventus" will be held at the Expo site on Poland's National Day, May 22.

The producer of this spectacular event is Director Andrzej Sulek of the Fryderyk

Chopin Institute and the Commissioner General of the Polish Section of Expo Slawomir Majman is the origins of this innovative project. The show has been created by the famous Polish composer Janusz Stoklosa fascinated by Chopin's music. Let's Dance Chopin's director and choreographer is Maria Stoklosa.

Polish Dragons Parade

When: 12:00 p.m. (noon) on May 22, 12:00 p.m. (noon) on May 23

Where: Expo, Bocheng Road

The legends of dragon are common in the Polish and Chinese culture and tradition. Polish dragons come from the medieval city of Krakow where the statue of Wawel Castle Dragon attracts thousands of visitors every year.

The Dragon's parade will be one of the main attractions of the Poland's National Day. 6 large-scale colorful balloons will appear over the Expo site in the parade along Bocheng Road. Don't miss the chance to take a picture with Polish Dragons!

Dance Action Show

When: 12:30 p.m. on May 22

Where: Expo, Europe Square

Polish Rozrywka Theatre's show will entertain the audience with different dance styles: contemporary, ballet, modern and hip-hop. The dancers' expressive movement will tell the story of social and cultural transitions including migration from villages to the cities. It will be a story of Poland and Silesia region translated into a universal language of dance and human body. Rozrywka Theatre dancers include finalists of the most popular TV dance show. Director of choreography is one of Poland's top artists, Piotr Jagielski.

Polish classical music played on traditional Chinese instruments

When: 11:00 a.m. on May 22

Where: Atrium Expo Centre (Official event)

Chinese Traditional Music Orchestra of Hangzhou Normal University's School of Music will present the audience a few creations of famous Polish composers: Fryderyk Chopin, Mieczyslaw Karlowicz, Jan Paderewski, Stanislaw Moniuszko, and a few Polish folk songs—all in marvelous arrangement, played on traditional Chinese instruments. The presentation of Polish music arranged and performed on traditional Chinese instruments is a tribute to thousand of years of Chinese music. The beauty of Polish music interpreted by great Chinese artists will be a feast for Chinese music lovers.

National Śląsk Song and Dance Ensemble

When: 6:30 p.m. on May 21, 6:00 p.m. on May 22

Where: Expo, Europe Square

Śląsk is one the most recognizable folk dance ensembles in the world. The performance showcase centuries-old Silesia folklore, Poland's most beautiful national songs and dances, among them the compositions of Frederic Chopin. The high artistic level of the ensemble has been recognized worldwide, bringing them numerous awards. Śląsk ensemble has frequently performed in all European capitals as well as in Africa, America, Australia and Asia. During the World Exhibition 2010 in Shanghai, Song and Dance Ensemble Śląsk will present concerts under the title "This is Poland".

Rock Jazz Chopin

When: 8:30 p.m., May 22

Where: Expo, Europe Square

The concert is an invitation to discover the music by Poland's most outstanding composer, Chopin, in an entirely new, contemporary context. For meeting young audience, we present rock and jazz versions of Chopin's work. During the performance, the audience will have an opportunity to compare them to the classical versions. The invited artists are outstanding interpreters whose performance has delighted the audience all over the world.

Sample 5   Poster of Shanghai Expo

Sample 6   Poster of a tourism festival

Sample 7   Tourism poster of Japan

Sample 8　Poster of a tour

Ⅲ. Useful Words and Expressions

ticket office 售票处

tourism sector 旅游（产）业，旅游部门

highlight v. 突出，强调

category n. 类别，种类

to revive tourism 振兴旅游业

to deal with crisis 应对危机

at the Expo site 在世博园区

dance show 舞蹈秀

feast n. 盛宴

press conference 记者招待会

former residence 故居

Credit Cards Accepted 可用信用卡支付

memorial n. 纪念馆

Children under 1 meter must be accompanied by an adult.

1米以下儿童须家长陪同乘坐。

Free for Children under 1.2 meters.

1.2米以下儿童免票。

Ⅳ. Sentence Examples

1. The meeting will be held in the conference room of the hotel at 10:00 a.m. on February 12, 2010. All managers are invited to attend.

兹定于2010年2月12日上午十点在酒店会议室召开会议,请各位经理参加。

2. The 10th Hangzhou West Lake Expo combined both Internet and "real" exhibitions to highlight the features of "enjoyment and experience".

第十届杭州西湖博览会将互联网与现实会展相结合,突出欣赏与体验特色。

3. The aim of this conference is to gain support from the international tourism industry, and restore the confidence of international markets in tourism in Sichuan after the earthquake.

本次会议旨在争取国际旅游界的支持,恢复国际市场对四川地震后旅游业的信心。

4. Don't miss the chance to take a picture with Polish Dragons!

千万不要错过拍摄波兰"龙的巡游"的好机会!

Ⅴ. Notes

1. the Beijing-Hangzhou Grand Canal 京杭大运河
2. the International Tourism Festival of the West Lake Expo 西湖博览会国际旅游节
3. the International Sister Cities' Mayors Summit 国际友好城市市长峰会
4. The General Assembly for Global Finance 全球金融大会
5. the First Suitable Living Festival 首届宜居生活节
6. the First Leisure and Shopping Festival of Hangzhou 首届杭州休闲购物节
7. the Performance Entertainment Expo 演出娱乐博览会
8. West Lake Expo on the Internet 网上西湖博览会
9. Poland Pavilion 世博会波兰馆
10. Polish National Day 世博会波兰馆日
11. Let's Dance Chopin "与肖邦共舞",波兰馆日活动之一
12. Polish Dragons Parade "龙的巡游",波兰馆日活动之一

Ⅵ. Practice

1. Translation.

①千万不要错过观看此次盛会的好机会!

②体验北京,走近奥运。

③The show will be a feast for music lovers in Shanghai.

④The aim of this conference is to revive the local tourism industry.

Chapter 2
Tourism Posters and Notices

2. Please write a notice of meeting according to the following information.

会议时间:2010 年 4 月 22 日 15:00

会议地点:旅行社三楼会议室

参加人员:各部门经理

Chapter 3

Letter Writing

Ⅰ. Introductions

An English letter consists of 8 components: letterhead, date, inside address, salutation, body of the letter, complimentary close, signature and enclosure. Below is the structure of a letter.

Heading

Inside Address

Salutation

(Body of Letter)

Complimentary Close

Signature

Enclosure

—Letterhead refers to the name and address of a person, a company or an institution printed as a heading. Address includes postcode and telephone number (optional), fax number, e-mail address, website address, and telex number.

Sometimes the letterhead also includes a logo.

——The date is placed on a single line one line below the letterhead. Letter format determines whether the date is flush with the right or left margin, a few spaces to right of center, or centered under the letterhead address.

a. Do not use figures for the month (11/12/2008)

b. The standard order of month and day (November 12, 2008) may be reversed and the comma omitted.

——The inside address is the recipient's address. Be sure to use an appropriate personal title (Mrs., Ms., Dr., etc.) and, if pertinent, use the business title (Director, Treasurer). If the business title is long (Director of Research Department), we can put it under the person's name.

——Salutation refers to the standard word or phrase used at the very beginning of a letter next to the person or firm being written to, i.e., "Dear Julia," "Dear Sirs,".

a. The person's or firm's name should agree with the name in the inside address. For example, if the letter is addressed to Dr. Carla Brown, the salutation should be "Dear Dr. Brown,", not "Dear Professor Brown,". If the letter is addressed to a firm, repeat the firm's name in the salutation: "Dear Sears & Roebuck Company,", or just use "Dear Sirs,".

b. The salutation is always flush left, two lines below the last line of the inside address. The salutation is generally followed by a colon in business correspondence and by a comma in personal letters.

——The complimentary close in a letter functions as a mark of both the end of the text and the respect for the address.

a. Remember to capitalize only the first letter of the complimentary close and always put a comma at the end. For example, "Sincerely," "Best wishes," "Yours sincerely,", etc.

b. The complimentary close is placed two lines below the text of the letter, either flush with the left margin (Block), aligned with the date (Modified Block), or a few spaces to the right of center (Indented).

c. Levels of formality

—Signature: An English letter always requires to be signed, whether it is formal or informal. The signature is aligned with, and four or five lines below, the complimentary close.

—Enclosure refers to thing or things put in an envelope with the letter. It serves both as a check to the recipient of the letter that everything was actually enclosed and as a reminder to the letter writer of what was sent.

a. The enclosure list is typed flush left, two spaces below the signature.

b. Some people prefer to use Encl. over Enclosure.

Ⅱ. Sample Reading

Sample 1　Letter for information requesting

P. O. Box 345
Shanghai Institute of Tourism
Shanghai, China
Postcode: 201103
March 12, 2010

San Francisco Travel

Agency, California

CA 95034

USA

Dear Sirs,

As I am planning to pay a visit to the city of San Francisco, California, I would like to request a package of tourist application materials. My desired time of entrance is December, 2010. I wish to have an enjoyable winter holiday.

I should also be obliged if you can send me the application forms and the relevant material at your earliest convenience.

Yours faithful,

Chang Heng

Sample 2 Letter for inquiring about tourist routes

P. O. Box 345

Shanghai Institute of Tourism

Shanghai, China

Postcode: 201103

March 12, 2010

Dear Sirs,

Messrs Brown Co. has advised us that you are promoting New Tours in South Africa. Would you please send us details and expenses of your new routes?

We are one of the most efficient Travel Groups Co. Ltd. in Shanghai. We believe that there will be a promising market in this area for moderately priced tours to your country.

We are looking forward to your early reply.

Yours faithful,

Chang Xin

Sample 3 Letter for booking a hotel room

GOLDEN TIGER IMP/EXP CO. LTD.

Add: 634 Yanqian Road, Jimei, Fujian, China

Tel: 0592-96089765

Fax: 0592-96089876

Postcode: 350000

June 30, 2010

Metropole Hotel

75 Waterloo Road

Kowloon, Hong Kong

China

Dear Sirs,

I would like to make a reservation for a Deluxe to accommodate Mr. Liu Xin, our President, from July 20 to 24, 2010.

Mr. Liu Xin will arrive in Hong Kong on July 20 and will pick up the reservation in the name of our company.

Yours sincerely,
Linda
(Secretary)

Sample 4   Meeting delay notification

Jeddah Travel Agency

688 Broadway Ave.

Jedda

April 26, 2010

Mr. Tom Brown

Harbor View Agency,

Malaysia

Mr. Brown,

I am sorry to inform you that the International Promotion Tour Conference has to be postponed till further notice because of a serious terrorist attack in the holding city. We would appreciate it very much if you could consider this and make some other arrangement in our behalf.

Yours sincerely,

W. Smith

Manager

Sample 5　Notice of route changing

Jeddah Travel Agency
688 Broadway Ave.
Jedda
April 26, 2010

Mr. Tom Brown

Harbor View Agency,

Malaysia

Mr. Brown,

Due to the typhoon that took place in the resort area that we have planned to visit, we find it very difficult to take your tour group as planned. I am writing this to you to suggest that we could change the original schedule until the conditions here are good enough to arrange tour groups. We would be grateful if you could consider all the above and inform the people concerned of this.

Yours sincerely,
Amy Liang
Manager

Sample 6 Invitation letter

March 26, 2017

Dear Professor Zeng,

On behalf of the Ohio State University and the IEEE Computer Society, I would be very pleased to invite you to attend and chair a session of the forthcoming 2017 International Conference on Parallel Data Processing to be held in Bellaire, Michigan, from August 25 to August 28, 2017.

You are an internationally acclaimed scholar and educator. Your participation will be among the highlights of the Conference.

We sincerely hope that you could accept our invitation. This is the 30th anniversary of the Conference and we plan to make it a truly international meeting. We have accepted many papers from several foreign countries, including two from your country.

We enclose a copy of the advanced program. If you like to come, please let us know as soon as possible, since we have to prepare this final program soon. We are looking forward to your acceptance.

Sincerely yours,

Peter

(signature)

Sample 7　Letter of thanks

June 1, 2016

Dear Mary,

I am writing this to express my thanks to you for the many kindnesses you showed me when I was in hospital.

If it had not been for your timely assistance, I am afraid that I would be still in hospital now. I got sick just a week before the exam. You treated me well and I recovered soon. Now I pass the exam. Without your kindness help, I would not have passed the exam.

Again, I would like to express my warm thanks to you. I shall be pleased to reciprocate your favor when the opportunity arises.

Yours sincerely,

Li Ming

Sample 8　Letter of congratulations

March 6, 2016

Dear Ruth,

I offer my warmest congratulations on your promotion to Vice President of the company. I know how talented you are and how hard you have worked to attain the goal. No one could have been more deserving. How exciting it must be for you to realize your ambitions after all those years of hard working! It is been a real encouragement to me to see your efforts rewarded.

Sincere congratulations to you. Your expertise and dedication will bring out the best of everyone on your staff. They are learning from a real professional.

I wish your further success.

Sincerely yours,

Tom Smith

Sample 9　Letter of complaints

Nov. 27, 2016

To whom it may concern,

I am writing to express my dissatisfaction with the service in your restaurant. On November 26, I dined with some friends at your restaurant. When we were there, no waitress or waiter actively served us. When we were about to order, they again ignored us, having small talk. When knowing we only ordered some set dinners, not the Thanksgiving turkey, the waitress called Jessie was rather arrogant and aggressive.

I really wish that you could pay more attention to your staff training and would never allow such a thing to happen again. Thank you for your time and consideration.

Yours Sincerely,

Raymond

Sample 10　Reply to a letter of complaints

Sunshine Holidays Ltd.

119 Sidney Street

London NW2 5CA

Mr Poul Nielsen

April 24, 2003

233 Sigurdsgade

Kebenhaven

Dear Mr. Nielsen,

We were very sorry to hear that the holiday on the island of Mocosa, organized by Sunshine Holidays, did not match your expectations.

Obviously, the fact that the flight from Luton was delayed by four hours was regrettable, certainly not due to any disorganization on behalf of Sunshine Holidays. Flight delays are often a frustrating part of flying, and tend to happen with increasing frequency at peak times like the Easter vacation.

The delay is probably the reason why you did not find a Sunshine representative at the airport to meet you. He had probably accompanied other tourists who had arrived at the airport. However, although this is an explanation, it is not an excuse, because you absolutely should have been met, and alternative arrangements should have been made. Sunshine Holidays deeply regrets the inconvenience you suffered through not being met at the airport and accompanied to your hotel. We will certainly look into the matter to make sure that it does not happen again, and of course we will reimburse you for the cost of taking a taxi.

I do not feel that we misrepresent the position of the hotel as the pictures of the "Beach Hotel" in our brochure show that it is on the cliffs and not on the beach, and there certainly was a bus service provided which you could have used if you did not want to walk. Many of our customers enjoy a 10 minutes' walk to the beach and back to get some exercise, and certainly enjoy the cliff views offered by the hotel. It is regrettable that the beach had litter on it. This is something that the local authorities should attend to, and we will notify them of your complaint.

Finally, as regards the facilities at the hotel, please rest assured that we will ask the hotel for explanations. The swimming pool should have been available. While the courier does not have control over the quality of the food, he should have passed on your complaints to the hotel management ponsonnel. The food is supposed to be typical of that region. It does not have great variety, but should be of good quality. When our staff went to check out the island before recommending it to customers, they found the food satisfactory.

Your satisfaction is our priority and we do appreciate your advice. So once again, please accept our apologies for the inconvenience that you suffered. Enclosed you will find reimbursement for the cost of the taxi, and also a discount voucher for your next holiday with our company. Thank you so much for bringing these things to our attention so that we can continually improve our service. We hope to see you and your wife again shortly.

Yours sincerely,
Bobby Fisher
Customer Relations Officer

III. Useful Words and Expressions

request n. 请求,索取

application form 申请表格

relevant adj. 相关的

obliged adj. 感激的

at your earliest convenience 尽早

promote v. 促销，增进

route n. 路线

promising adj. 有前景的

moderately priced tour 价格合适的旅行

deluxe suite 豪华套房

in the name of 以……的名义

atmosphere n. 气氛，氛围

reciprocate v. 回报

to match one's expectations 达到某人的期望

at peak times 在高峰期

flight delay 航班延迟

off-season vacation 淡季出行

leaflet n. 传单，散页印刷品

FW(farword) 转发

CC(carbon copy) 抄送

BCC(blind carbon copy) 密送

Conf(confidential) 保密

BTW(By the way) 顺便提一下

ASAP(as soon as possible) 尽快

FYI(for your information) 请参考

Ⅳ. Sentence Examples

1. As I am planning to pay a visit to the city of San Francisco, California, I would

like to request a package of tourist application materials.

本人拟到加利福尼亚州旧金山市旅游,今特致函索取有关旅游方面的申请材料。

2. I should be obliged if you can send me the application forms and the relevant material at your earliest convenience.

如能尽快给我寄来申请表格及相关材料,我将十分感激。

3. Would you please send us details and expenses of your new routes?

请寄送新线路的详细安排及价格。

4. We are looking forward to your early reply.

盼尽早答复。

5. We believe that there will be a promising market in this area for moderately priced tours to your country.

如果价格合适,定会有大量游客前往参观。

6. I whould like to make a reservation for a Deluxe to accommodate Mr. Liu Xin.

兹致函为刘新先生预订一套豪华套房。

7. I am sorry to inform you that the International Promotion Tour Conference has to be postponed till further notice because of...

我非常遗憾地通知您,由于……,国际旅游促进大会不得不延期举行,何时召开另行通知。

8. We would be grateful if you could consider all the above and inform the people concerned of this.

如能谅解并通知相关人员,我们将非常感激。

9. You are cordially invited to the reception.

我们热忱地期待您能莅临此次招待会。

10. I hope you will be able to join us on November 7.

期待您能于11月7日光临。

11. Your warm hospitality will remain fresh in my memory for a long time.

您的热情好客,令我久久难以忘怀。

12. I am writing to complain about a holiday organized by your travel agency.

在此，我对由贵旅行社组织的一次旅行进行投诉。

13. You can start an email with the following sentences:

—I hope everything goes well with you.

—I believe that you must have enjoyed your holiday in Japan.

—Thank you for contacting us.

—Thank you for your prompt(及时的) reply.

—Thank you for getting back to me.

—Thank you for providing the requested information.

—Thank you for all your assistance.

—I truly appreciate your help in resolving the problem.

—Thank you for your feedback.

14. You can conclude an email/letter with the sentences below:

—I look forward to hearing from you soon.

—I look forward to meeting / seeing you next Tuesday.

—Please contact us if we can help.

—Please do not hesitate to contact me if there is any problem.

—Thank you for your kind cooperation.

—Thank you for your attention to this matter.

—Thank you for your understanding.

—Thank you for your consideration.

—Thank you again for everything you have done.

Ⅴ. Notes

1. day-to-day activities 日常事务

2. San Francisco, California 美国加利福尼亚州旧金山市

3. on top of everything 更过分的是，更重要的是

4. a full or partial refund 全部或部分退款

5. reimburse 赔偿。例：We will reimburse you for your traveling expenses. 我们将赔偿您的旅费。

6. as regards 关于，至于。例：I have little information as regards his past. 我对他过去的情况不太了解。

7. a discount voucher 打折优惠券

Ⅵ. Practice

1. Translation.

①如能谅解我方困境，我们将不胜感激。

②希望您早日回复。

③We were very sorry to hear that the holiday on the island did not match your expectations.

④Due to the typhoon that took place in the resort area that we have planned to visit, we find it very difficult to take your tour group here as planned.

2. Please write an invitation letter according to the following instructions.

复旦大学外文学院王芳想写封邀请信给上海市大连西路 550 号上海外国语大学英语系的刘梅教授，邀请她于 2016 年 10 月 24 日星期一下午 6:00 在学校大礼堂做题为"如何用英语有效交流"的讲座，并请她回复是否能做讲座。

3. Please write a letter of thanks according to the following instructions.

你在饭店吃午饭时丢失钱包，写信给你下榻的宾馆经理，感谢饭店员工王小姐拾金不昧。

Chapter 4

Itineraries

Ⅰ. Introductions

An itinerary is a detailed schedule or a suggested route for a journey. When a delegation or a person pays a visit, an itinerary is usually to be made, including the time to set out and return, the route of visit, the dwelling place, the main contents of the visit, etc. With the help of an itinerary, a traveler can maximize his or her potential, avoid regrettable changes and make the best of the trip. An itinerary should be:

1. clear.
2. simple.
3. detailed.

Ⅱ. Sample Reading

Sample 1

Trip Itinerary

Shanghai→ Los Angeles→ Las Vegas→ Shanghai

Day	Date	City	Touring Spots	Accommodation	Transportation
1	2018/12/19 (Wed)	Shanghai→Los Angeles	By air from Shanghai to Los Angeles	La Quinta Inn & Suites LAX	Flight 3U8689 Shanghai → Los Angeles 13:55-20:40
2	2018/12/20 (Thu)	Los Angeles→ San Diego→Los Angeles	Port of San Diego, Victory Kiss, USS Midway Museum, Balboa Park	La Quinta Inn & Suites LAX	By bus
3	2018/12/21 (Fri)	Los Angeles	Hollywood Walk of Fame, TCL Chinese Theatre, Dolby Theatre, Universal Studios Hollywood	La Quinta Inn & Suites LAX	By bus

续表

Day	Date	City	Touring Spots	Accommodation	Transportation
4	2018/12/22 (Sat)	Los Angeles→Barstow	By bus from Los Angeles to Barstow	Embassy Suites by Hilton Convention Center Las Vegas	Bus Los Angeles → Barstow
		Barstow	Outlets at Barstow		By walk
		Barstow→Las Vegas	By bus from Barstow to Las Vegas		Bus Barstow→Las Vegas
5	2018/12/23 (Sun)	Las Vegas	Grand Canyon	Embassy Suites by Hilton Convention Center Las Vegas	By bus
6	2018/12/24 (Mon)	Las Vegas→Los Angeles	Beverly Hills, Farmers Market	Holiday Inn Los Angeles LAX Airport	Bus Las Vegas→Los Angeles
7	2018/12/25 (Tue)	Los Angeles	Walt Disney Concert Hall, Los Angels City Hall, Staples Center, University Of California, Los Angeles, Santa Monica Beach	Holiday Inn Los Angeles→LAX Airport	By bus

Chapter 4
Itineraries

续表

Day	Date	City	Touring Spots	Accommodation	Transportation
8	2018/12/26 (Wed)	Los Angeles	Desert Hills Premium Outlets	Holiday Inn Los Angeles→LAX Airport	By bus
9	2018/12/27 (Thu)	Los Angeles→Shanghai	By air from Los Angeles to Shanghai	Check out the hotel	Flight 3U8700 Los Angeles→Shanghai 00:55-06:00+1
10	2018/12/28 (Fri)	Shanghai	18:10 Arrive at Putong International Airport	END	

Remarks:

La Quinta Inn & Suites LAX

Address: 5249 West Century Boulevard, Los Angeles, CA 90045, USA

Embassy Suites by Hilton Convention Center Las Vegas

Address: 3600 Paradise Road, Las Vegas, NV 89169, USA

Holiday Inn Los Angeles-LAX Airport:

Address: 9901 South La Cienega Boulevard, Los Angeles, CA 90045, USA

Sample 2

Itinerary For European Tourists
May 6-8, 2019, Beijing

Note: All times are local times.

Hotel addresses, phone numbers and the charges are on attached sheet.

MONDAY MAY 6 (Arrive in Beijing)

10:50 a.m. Arrive at the Beijing Capital Airport

(Air China Flight CA981)

11:30 a.m. Lunch time

(Beijing Jindingxuan Cantonese Restaurant)

14:00 p.m. The sight seeing tour to visit the Temple of Heaven

17:30 p.m. Welcome dinner

18:30 p.m. Beijing Opera

(Beijing Quanjude Roast Duck Restaurant)

20:00 p.m. Drive you back to hotel, free on your own

(Capital Hotel)

TUESDAY MAY 7 (Beijing Sight-seeing)

7:00 a.m. Breakfast in the hotel

8:00 a.m. Pick you up at your hotel

(Full day tour to visit the Great Wall at Badaling and Ming Tombs)

11:30 a.m. Lunch time

(Beijing Jindingxuan Cantonese Restaurant)

17:30 p.m. Dinner

(Beijing Quanjude Roast Duck Restaurant)

18:30 p.m. Drive you back to hotel, free on your own

(Capital Hotel)

WEDNESDAY MAY 8 (Beijing Sight-seeing and depart)

7:00 a.m. Breakfast in the hotel

8:00 a.m. Pick you up at your hotel

9:00 a.m. Visit the Tian'anmen Square, Forbidden City, Summer Palace

11:30 a.m. <u>Lunch time</u>

         (Beijing Wahaha Restaurant)

15:00 p.m. <u>Beijing Airport see-off service and end the Beijing trip</u>

         (Air China Fight CA982)

Cost inclusion:

1. Transportation: Private air-conditioned car, van or bus and driver.

2. Guide: Private English tour guide.

3. Meals: Daily breakfast at the hotel, Chinese lunch & dinner in local Chinese restaurant as indicated in the itinerary.

4. Entry fees: The main entrance tickets for the sight-seeing spots and entertainment mentioned.

5. Free two bottles of mineral water for every day.

Sample 3

2-Day New York to Niagara Falls and Thousand Islands Tour

DAY1 New York - Niagara Falls

Departing from New York, we head for Niagara Falls to experience its majesty. It is the most powerful waterfall in North America, with an average of 112000 cubic meters of water falls over the crest every minute. A historical boat ride aboard the world-famous **Maid of the Mist** offers up close and exciting views of the Falls (**seasonal**). A visit to **IMAX Niagara Falls** also awaits us. Home to "The Falls Movie: Legends and Daredevils", the **IMAX** provides a glimpse into the stories of the courageous few who dared to climb into a barrel and tumble down the powerful Falls. There is also the **Cave of the Winds**, which brings you closer to the waters of Niagara Falls than ever (**optional**). After an elevator ride deep into the Niagara Gorge, a series of wooden walkways lead to the hurricane deck—a mere 20 feet from the towering Bridal Veil Falls. At night, we are treated to the spectacular night time views of Niagara Falls, where every evening the Falls are lit in the colors of the rainbow. The lighting of the Falls, which has a 140-year-old tradition, allows visitors to enjoy the beauty of the mighty Niagara clearly even at night.

DAY2 Niagara Falls-Thousand Islands-New York

Leaving Niagara Falls, the tour then proceeds to the **Thousand Islands**. Situated between the U.S. and Canadian border are 1793 islands on the Saint Lawrence River, considered the fresh water boating capital of the world. The water, even 80 feet deep, is so clear in some areas that a rocky bottom can be seen. Because of the great number of rocks and shoals just above or below the water's surface, it is difficult to travel on the waters at night. Luckily, we will have an opportunity to take a leisure boat cruise along the river (**seasonal**), which includes unique sights such as the world's smallest international bridge. The tour will then return to New York.

Itineraries are subject to change so that we can provide you with the best possible experience.

Inclusions:

One-night hotel accommodation.

Roundtrip transportation via air-conditioned, lavatory-equipped motor coaches.

Tour guide (Level 2: semi-guided tour).

Exclusions:

Laundry, valet, telephone calls, wines and liquors other than those specified.

All meals and drinks during the trip. And the tour guide will arrange for the details.

All admission fee and all other private expenses. Service Fees for tour guide/bus driver ($6 per day per person).

Chapter 4
Itineraries

Additional Information:

Single price is for one person staying in one room. Double, Triple and Quad prices are for two people, three people and four people staying in one room respectively.

Language:

All tours are escorted by professional bilingual or multi-lingual tour and/or driver guides (English/Chinese). Depending on the number of passengers booked for a particular departure, tours and/or languages may be combined to operate the tours.

Sample 4

Five Days Beijing and Xi'an Tour Package

Day 1 Beijing Arrival

Arrive at Beijing Airport, meet and transfer to the fixed hotel.

Day 2 (B, L, D)

Full day trip to Tian'anmen Square, Forbidden City, silk store, Temple of Heaven and Summer Palace. In the evening (7:15-8:30 p.m.), after dinner, enjoy Chinese Acrobatic show.

Tian'anmen Square: The largest city square in the world.

Forbidden City: The largest imperial palace in China during the Ming and Qing dynasties with a history of around 600 years.

Visit scenic spots: ①The Hall and the Courtyard of Supreme Harmony; ②The Meridian Gate; ③The Hall of Supreme Harmony; ④The Hall of Complete Harmony; ⑤The Hall of Preserving Harmony; ⑥The Huge Stone Carving; ⑦The Hall of Union; ⑧The Palace of Earthly Tranquility; ⑨The Imperial Garden, etc.

Temple of Heaven: The place where the ancient emperors used to pray for the God's blessings on the whole nation.

Visit scenic spots: ①The Hall of Prayer for good harvest; ②Red Stairway Bridge; ③The Imperial Vault of Heaven; ④The Echo Wall; ⑤Triple-sound Stone; ⑥The Circular Mound Altar, etc.

Summer Palace: The largest and best-preserved royal garden in China with a history of over 800 years.

Visit scenic spots: ①East Palace Gate; ②The Hall of Benevolence and Longevity; ③Hall of Jade Billows; ④The Hall of Joyful Longevity; ⑤The Covered Walkway; ⑥The Marble Boat, etc.

Day 3 (B, L, D)

Full day trip to the Great Wall, Ming Tomb, jade market and Sacred Road. Enjoy a Peking Duck Banquet for dinner in the famous Quanjude Restaurant.

Great Wall: One of the seven wonders in the world and the symbol of China (60 miles away from downtown, about one and half an hours' drive).

Visit scenic spots: Badaling Geat Wall, Badaling Fortress, Beacon-Towers, "Looking-toward Beijing Stone", etc.

Ming Tombs: The only underground tomb of the thirteen tombs of the emperors in the Ming Dynasty.

Visit scenic spots: ①Ling'en Gate; ②Ling'en Palace; ③Soul Tower; ④The Great Red Gate; ⑤The Stele Pavilion, etc.

Sacred Road: The road is guarded on both sides with stone statues by which the ancient emperors went to hold memorial ceremonies for the ancestors.

Day 4 (B, L) Beijing→Xi'an→Beijing

Transfer you to airport to take morning flight at around 7:30 for Xi'an.

Upon arrival, meet at airport and transfer to visit Terra-cotta Warriors and Ancient City Wall with lunch included.

Transfer back to airport for you to take late afternoon flight at 6:00 p.m.

Beijing driver will fetch you back to hotel.

Day 5 (B) Beijing Departure

Transfer from hotel to airport or railway station, see-off.

Price Includes:

(1) Private ground transfer along the schedule, and sight entrance tickets.

(2) Meals as listed in the itinerary, B=breakfast, L=lunch, D=Dinner.

(3) Personal English speaking tour guide explains sight-seeings along the tour.

(4) Hotel accommodations (twin share or triple room) as listed in the itinerary.

(5) All service charges and taxes.

(6) Inter flights between Beijing and Xi'an.

Ⅲ. Useful Words and Expressions

1. Fly to Beijing in the morning and visit the Summer Palace in the afternoon.

早上乘飞机前往北京,下午参观颐和园。

2. This itinerary is open to adjustments.

本次行程允许变更。

3. Chengdu to Shanghai by flight, stay in a four-star hotel.

乘飞机从成都前往上海,入住四星级酒店。

4. After breakfast at the hotel, the tour will be finished.

酒店早餐后,旅程结束。

5. Please go to the airport by your own means of transportation.

请自行前往机场。

6. You are going to inspect Economic and Technological Development Zone this afternoon.

今天下午您将视察经济技术开发区。

7. The meeting was called to order by Zhang Ming at 10:30 a.m..

上午 10:30 张明宣布会议开始。

8. Participants included...

参会人员包括……

9. The next meeting was provisionally arranged on Thursday, July 18.

下次会议暂定在 7 月 18 日,星期四。

10. The next regular meeting is scheduled on May 15, at 2:30 p.m..

下次常务会议定于 5 月 15 日下午 2:30 召开。

11. The meeting was adjourned at 4:00 p.m..

下午四点会议结束。

12. round table 圆桌会议

13. tentative itinerary 暂定的旅行计划

14. leave...for... 离开某地去……

15. transfer to the hotel 转至宾馆

16. return to Conference Venue 返回会议举办地点

17. depart from... 从……出发

18. depart for... 前往……

19. check-in 入住登记

20. check-out 退房结账

21. room registration 登记房间

22. a matter of high priority 非常需要优先考虑的事情

23. introduction and welcome remarks 介绍和欢迎致词

24. coffee break 休息

25. close and departure 闭幕离开

Ⅳ. Sentence Examples

1. Leaving Niagara Falls, the tour then proceeds to...

离开尼亚加拉瀑布,然后继续前往……

2. Departing from New York, we head for ...

从纽约出发,我们前往……

3. Situated between the U.S. and Canadian border are ...

位于美国和加拿大边界之间的是……

4. We will have an opportunity to ...

我们将有机会……

5. The tour will then return to ...

旅程随后将回到……

6. It allows visitors to enjoy ...

它使游客享受到……

7. We are treated to ...

我们受到款待……

8. After an elevator ride, ...

乘电梯后,……

9. It brings you closer to ...

它让你更接近……

10. During your San Francisco tour, you will be provided with in-depth historical narrative about...

在您的旧金山之旅中,您将会看到关于……的深入历史叙述。

Ⅴ. Notes

因行程表和议程表在活动安排上要求时间、地点、事件准确,在写作时通常要注意以下几点:

①明确团体或个人出发和到达的日期和时间。为避免混淆,常常使用 24 小时制计

时方法。若过程中出现时差情况,应当标注是否为当地时间。

②若某一城市中有不只一个机场或车站,应将出发和抵达的机场名称或车站名称标示清楚。

③须指明交通方式。若乘坐飞机,需要说明航空公司和航班班次;若乘坐火车,需说明车次。

④提供住宿的详细情况,如宾馆详细地址、联系电话、房间类型(单间、双人间、套房等)、房间号、餐饮情况等也应一并标注。

Ⅵ. Practice

1. Write subtitles based on the sentences:

Example: In the morning, we will visit the Battle of the Bulge Museum.

Morning: Battle of the Bulge Museum

(1) Afternoon: American cemetery and meeting with a woman survivor of World War Ⅱ

(2) Morning: Chocolate tasting

(3) Morning: Guided walk in the Heart of Brussels

(4) Afternoon: Free time for shopping or museums

2. Rewrite the following sentences:

(1) After a welcome reception and orientation meeting, you will have your first Belgian dinner.

(2) We will visit the Battle of the Bulge Museum at the Bastogne Historical Center which will allow you to relive moments of the battle and a day in the life of an American soldier.

(3) The 90-acre cemetery contains the graves of 5329 of US soldiers.

(4) After this emotional visit, we will spend some time with a woman, a survivor

of the war, who will open her house to us.

(5) We will leave our guesthouse and head off for another one near Brugge. On the way, we will stop by a local chocolate maker.

(6) One of our best stops of San Francisco!

3. Translate the following sentences into English.

(1) 您将乘飞机从北京前往重庆，入住四星级酒店。

(2) 布莱克先生和史密斯小姐需要接机，并乘车至假日旅馆。

(3) 所有参会人员将乘车前往会议举办地点。

(4) 会议将于下午六点前结束。

4. Write an itinerary based on the following draft.

Entry Beijing

Our guide will hold a welcome sign to meet you outside the baggage claim area at the Beijing Capital Airport according to your international (internal) flight schedule. Transfer to the 4-star hotel for 2 nights stay and relax for the rest of the day.

Meals: We do not arrange any meals for you today because we have different arrival flights.

Hotel: Holiday Inn Central Plaza—the best Holiday Inn Hotel in Beijing (4-star).

Beijing

Morning excursion transfers you to climb the Great Wall—Badaling section. A spicy Sichuan cuisine lunch is served at a notable restaurant to restore your physical energy. In the afternoon, stroll across the Sacred Road and reach the Ming Tombs. On the way back to downtown, we will drive by the Bird's Nest (National Olympic Stadium). You will see its appearance at a distance.

Meals: Breakfast, Lunch

Descriptions:

Great Wall: Without any modern communication facilities, the information transportation along the Great Wall just depended on the dense beacon towers which were built every 2.5 kilometers to 5 kilometers. From the Han Dynasty, the complex codes for alarm signals were listed as the nation's top secret. There are mainly two methods to transmit information—heavy smoke was used in daytime and bonfire was used at night. At the early time, waving bright flags and beating drums for warning and communication were also adopted by soldiers.

Beijing-Pingyao

Stroll along the famous Tian'anmen Square (the largest square in the world), and reach the Forbidden City. Lunch is served at a very nice restaurant, and you can taste the authentic Chinese food. In the afternoon, transfer to visit the Temple of Heaven. Ride a soft sleeper train to Pingyao.

Meals: Breakfast, Lunch

Hotel: An overnight soft sleeper train

Descriptions:

Tian'anmen Square: Between the Tian'anmen Square and the Imperial Palace, there are five Golden Water Bridges well sculptured of white marble. The midmost Imperial Bridge, which is 8.55 meters wide and engraved with dragon, was for the exclusive use of the ancient emperors. The two 5.78-meter-wide bridges on both sides were constructed for the royal family and so called the Royal's Bridges. The outmost two bridges were called the Ministerial Bridges, both of which are 4.55 meters wide and were used by the civil military officials above the third rank.

Forbidden City: The Forbidden City has four gates in four directions. The south is the Meridian Gate, the north is the Divine Prowess Gate, the east is the Donghua Gate, and the west is the Xihua Gate. Among these four gates, the Meridian Gate is the frontispiece, where the emperor issued proclamations and gave orders to the army. When the emperor announced proclamations, all the civil and military officials should assemble at the square in front of the Meridian Gate and listened orders very carefully. The entrance in the middle of the Meridian Gate is especially prepared for emperors.

Pingyao

The local guide will wait for you at Pingyao Railway Station ahead of the train schedule and transfer you to hotel. After breakfast at the hotel, you will touch Pingyao by visiting the Ming-Qing Street, the Chenghuang Temple, the Ri Sheng Chang Exchange Shop and the Tongxinggong Ancient Bank Safeguard. Then visit the City Wall in Pingyao ancient town.

Meals: Breakfast, Lunch

Hotel: Yide Guest House

Descriptions:

Ancient Ming-Qing Street: As one of the notable attractions in Pingyao, the Ancient Ming-Qing Street, also named the South Street, was the prosperous commercial center of the county. In this 750-meter-long ancient street, there are hundreds of various stores selling groceries, silks and medicine.

Pingyao-Taiyuan-Beijing

Continue to tour Pingyao by visiting the Shuanglin Monastery and have a stop at Qiao Family's Compound. Drive back to Taiyuan. Jinci Temple visit will be arranged on the way. Take an overnight soft sleeper train back to Beijing.

Meals: Breakfast, Lunch

Hotel: An overnight soft sleeper train

Descriptions:

Qiao Family's Compound: Located in the Qixian County in Shanxi Province, the Qiao Family's Compound is 54 kilometers away from Taiyuan. Also named the Zaizhong Hall, the compound was the well-known capitalist Qiao Zhiyong's residence. Originally built during the Emperor Qianlong's reign in the Qing Dynasty, it has been restored for several times. Now the majestic complexes represent the unique architectural style of the residence in North China during the Qing Dynasty.

Shuanglin Temple: The Shuanglin Temple lies in the southwest part of Pingyao, covering an area of 15000 square meters. The temple is composed of two parts, the East and the West Parts. The main constructions are in the West Part, including ten halls, namely the Shijia Hall, Luohan Hall, Wusheng Hall, Tudi Hall, Yanluo Hall, Tianwang Hall, Main Hall (Daxiong Baodian), Qianfo (Thousand Buddha) Hall, Buddha Hall, Niangniang (Queen Mother) Hall and Zhenyi Hall.

Jinci Temple: Being 25 kilometers far from Taiyuan, the Jinci Temple was considered as the most famous attraction of the city. Built in the Northern Wei Dynasty, the temple was in memory of Ji Yu, the second son of King Wu of the Zhou Dynasty (the second emperor of the Zhou Dynasty). The expansion and reconstruction to the temple lasted for the later Sui, Tang, Song, Yuan, Ming and Qing dynasties.

Beijing

The local guide will wait for you at the railway station ahead of the train schedule and transfer you to the hotel. Have the breakfast at the hotel and relax in the morning. Visit the Summer Palace and the Lama Temple after lunch.

Specials: Peking Roast Duck Banquet and Chinese Kung Fu Show at Red Theatre

Meals: Breakfast, Lunch, Dinner

Hotel: Holiday Inn Central Plaza—the best Holiday Inn Hotel in Beijing (4-star)

Descriptions:

Summer Palace: The Summer Palace is known as an entertainment place for emperors during the Qing Dynasty (1644-1911). But there is also administrative area for emperors inside the park. The place is called the Hall of Benevolence and Longevity (Renshoudian). There you will experience the emperors' administrative life by viewing the furnishings remained in the hall, such as a platform with a throne furnished with nine dragons, the delicate peacock-feather fans, a monster-shaped censer, and an elaborate red sandalwood screen.

Lama Temple: The Lama Temple, also known as Yong He Palace in China, is noted not only for its profound Tibetan religious culture, but also for its inseparable relationship with the emperors of the Qing Dynasty. From 1694 to 1722, it is the dwelling of the Emperor Yongzheng. He was the fourth prince of Emperor Kangxi and came to the throne in 1722. During this period, another emperor of the Qing Dynasty was also born here, who is the fourth son of Yongzheng—the Emperor Qianlong.

Beijing Exit

Private transfer takes you to the airport, and your pleasant China tour ends here.

Meals: Breakfast

5. Write an itinerary for a two-day tour of your favorite city.

Chapter 5

Application Forms in Tourism Industry

Ⅰ. Introductions

Forms are often used to collect information. Usually, personal details are requested in forms in tourism industry. When filling in the form, read the filling requirements carefully, and make sure that the handwriting is neat and the content is true and clear.

Ⅱ. Sample Reading

Sample 1

Form V. 2013

中华人民共和国签证申请表
Visa Application Form of the People's Republic of China
（For the Mainland of China only）

申请人必须如实、完整、清楚地填写本表格。请逐项在空白处用中文或英文大写字母打印填写，或在□内打√选择。如有关项目不适用，请写"无"。**The applicant should fill in this form truthfully, completely and clearly. Please type the answer in capital English letters in the space provided or tick（√）the relevant box to select. <u>If some of the items do not apply, please type N/A or None.</u>**

一、个人信息 Part 1: Personal Information

1.1 英文姓名 Full English name as in passport	姓 Last name		粘贴一张近期正面免冠、浅色背景的彩色护照照片。 <u>照片/Photo</u> Affix one recent color passport photo (full face, front view, bareheaded and against a plain light colored background).
	中间名 Middle name		
	名 First name		
1.2 中文姓名 Name in Chinese		1.3 别名或曾用名 Other name(s)	
1.4 性别 Sex □ 男 M □ 女 F		1.5 出生日期 DOB(yyyy-mm-dd)	

续表

1.6 现有国籍 Current nationality(ies)	1.7 曾有国籍 Former nationality(ies)
1.8 出生地点(市、省/州、国) Place of birth(city, Province/state, country)	
1.9 身份证/公民证号码 Local ID/ Citizenship number	
1.10 护照/旅行证件种类 Passport/Travel document type	☐ 外交 Diplomatic　☐ 公务、官员 Service or Official ☐ 普通 Ordinary　☐ 其他证件(请说明) Other (Please specify):
1.11 护照号码 Passport number	1.12 签发日期 Date of issue(yyyy-mm-dd)
1.13 签发地点 Place of issue	1.14 失效日期 Date of expiry(yyyy-mm-dd)
1.15 当前职业 (可选多项) Current occupation(s)	☐ 商人 Businessperson ☐ 公司职员 Company employee ☐ 演艺人员 Entertainer ☐ 工人/农民 Industrial/Agricultural worker ☐ 学生 Student ☐ 乘务人员 Crew member ☐ 自雇 Self-employed ☐ 无业 Unemployed ☐ 退休 Retired ☐ 前/现任议员 Former/incumbent member of parliament 　职位 Position _____ ☐ 前/现任政府官员 Former/incumbent government official 　职位 Position _____ ☐ 军人 Military personnel 　职位 Position _____ ☐ 非政府组织人员 NGO staff ☐ 宗教人士 Religious personnel ☐ 新闻从业人员 Staff of media ☐ 其他(请说明) Other (Please specify):

续表

1.16 受教育程度 Education	☐ 研究生 Postgraduate　　　　　　　　☐ 大学 College ☐ 其他（请说明）Other (Please specify)：	
1.17 工作单位/学校 Employer/School	名称 Name	联系电话 Phone number
	地址 Address	邮政编码 Zip Code
1.18 家庭住址 Home address		1.19 邮政编码 Zip Code
1.20 电话/手机 Home/mobile phone number		1.21 电子邮箱 E-mail address
1.22 婚姻状况 Marital status	☐ 已婚 Married　　☐ 单身 Single　　☐ 其他 Other (Please specify)：			

	姓名 Name	国籍 Nationality	职业 Occupation	关系 Relationship
1.23 主要家庭成员（配偶、子女、父母等，可另纸）Major family members (spouse, children, parents, etc., may type on separate paper)				

续表

1.24 紧急联络人信息 Emergency Contact	姓名 Name	手机 Mobile phone number
	与申请人的关系 Relationship with the applicant	

1.25 申请人申请签证时所在的国家或地区 Country or territory where the applicant is located when applying for this visa	

二、旅行信息 Part 2: Travel Information

2.1 申请入境事由 Major purpose of your visit	☐ 官方访问 Official Visit ☐ 旅游 Tourism ☐ 交流、考察、访问 Non-business visit ☐ 商业贸易 Business & Trade ☐ 人才引进 As introduced talent ☐ 执行乘务 As crew member ☐ 过境 Transit	☐ 常驻外交、领事、国际组织人员 As resident diplomat, consul or staff of international organization ☐ 永久居留 As permanent resident ☐ 工作 Work ☐ 寄养 As child in foster care
	☐ 短期探望中国公民或者具有中国永久居留资格的外国人 Short-term visit to Chinese citizen or foreigner with Chinese permanent residence status	☐ 与中国公民或者具有中国永久居留资格的外国人家庭团聚居留超过180日 Family reunion for over 180 days with Chinese citizen or foreigner with Chinese permanent residence status
	☐ 短期探望因工作、学习等事由在中国停留居留的外国人 Short-term visit to foreigner residing in China due to work, study or other reasons	☐ 长期探望因工作、学习等事由在中国居留的外国人 As accompanying family member of foreigner residing in China due to work, study or other reasons

续表

2.1 申请入境事由 Major purpose of your visit	☐ 短期学习 Short-term study for less than 180 days	☐ 长期学习 Long-term study for over 180 days
	☐ 短期采访报道 As journalist for temporary news coverage	☐ 外国常驻中国新闻机构记者 As resident journalist
	☐ 其他（请说明）Other（Please specify）：	
2.2 计划入境次数 Intended number of entries	☐ 一次（自签发之日起 3 个月有效）One entry valid for 3 months from the date of issue ☐ 二次（自签发之日起 3—6 个月有效）Two entries valid for 3 to 6 months from the date of issue ☐ 半年多次（自签发之日起 6 个月有效）Multiple entries valid for 6 months from the date of issue ☐ 一年多次（自签发之日起 1 年有效）Multiple entries valid for 1 year from the date of issue ☐ 其他（请说明）Other（Please specify）：	
2.3 是否申请加急服务 Are you applying for express service? 注：加急服务须经领事官员批准，将加收费用。Note: Express service needs approval of consular officials, and extra fees may apply.	☐ 是 Yes ☐ 否 No	
2.4 本次行程预计首次抵达中国的日期 Expected date of your first entry into China on this trip （yyyy-mm-dd）		

续表

2.5 预计行程中单次在华停留的最长天数 **Longest intended stay in China among all entries**		Days

	日期 Date	详细地址 Detailed address
2.6 在中国境内行程（按时间顺序，可附另纸填写） **Itinerary in China (in time sequence, may type on separate paper)**		

2.7 谁将承担在中国期间的费用？Who will pay for your travel and expenses during your stay in China?	

	姓名或名称 Name	
2.8 中国境内邀请单位或个人信息 **Information of inviter in China**	地址 Address	
	联系电话 Phone number	
	与申请人关系 Relationship with the applicant	

2.9 是否曾经获得过中国签证？如有，请说明最近一次获得中国签证的时间和地点。Have you ever been granted a Chinese visa? If applicable, please specify the date and place of the last time you were granted the visa.	
2.10 过去12个月中访问的其他国家或地区 Other countries or territories you visited in the last 12 months	

三、其他事项 Part 3: Other Information

3.1 是否曾在中国超过签证或居留许可允许的期限停留？Have you ever overstayed your visa or residence permit in China?	☐是 Yes	☐否 No
3.2 是否曾经被拒绝签发中国签证，或被拒绝进入中国？Have you ever been refused a visa for China, or been refused entry into China?	☐是 Yes	☐否 No
3.3 是否在中国或其他国家有犯罪记录？Do you have any criminal record in China or any other country?	☐是 Yes	☐否 No
3.4 是否具有以下任一种情形 Are you experiencing any of the following conditions? ①严重精神障碍 Serious mental disorder ②传染性肺结核病 Infectious pulmonary tuberculosis ③可能危害公共卫生的其他传染病 Other infectious disease of public health hazards	☐是 Yes	☐否 No
3.5 近 30 日内是否前往过流行性疾病传染的国家或地区？Did you visit countries or territories affected by infectious diseases in the last 30 days?	☐是 Yes	☐否 No
3.6 如果对 3.1 到 3.5 的任何一个问题选择"是"，请在下面详细说明。 If you select Yes to any questions from 3.1 to 3.5, please give details below.		
3.7 如果有本表未涉及而需专门陈述的其他与签证申请相关的事项，请在此或另纸说明。 If you have more information about your visa application other than the above to declare, please give details below or type on a separate paper.		
3.8 如申请人护照中的偕行人与申请人一同旅行，请将偕行人照片粘贴在下面并填写偕行人信息。If someone else travels and shares the same passport with the applicant, please affix their photos and give their information below.		

续表

偕行人信息 Information	偕行人 1 Person 1 粘贴照片于此 Affix Photo here	偕行人 2 Person 2 粘贴照片于此 Affix Photo here	偕行人 3 Person 3 粘贴照片于此 Affix Photo here
姓名 Full name			
性别 Sex			
生日 DOB(yyyy-mm-dd)			

四、声明及签名 Part 4: Declaration & Signature

4.1 我声明,我已阅读并理解此表所有内容要求,并愿就所填报信息和申请材料的真实性承担一切法律后果。

I hereby declare that I have read and understood all the questions in this application and shall bear all the legal consequences for the authenticity of the information and materials I provided.

4.2 我理解,能否获得签证、获得何种签证、入境次数以及有效期、停留期等将由领事官员决定,任何不实、误导或填写不完整均可能导致签证申请被拒绝或被拒绝进入中国。

I understand that whether to issue a visa, type of visa, number of entries, validity and duration of each stay will be determined by consular official, and that any false, misleading or incomplete statement may result in the refusal of a visa for or denial of entry into China.

续表

4.3 我理解,根据中国法律,申请人即使持有中国签证仍有可能被拒绝入境。

I understand that, according to Chinese law, applicant may be refused entry into China even if a visa is granted.

➡ 申请人签名   日期

Applicant's signature: _____   Date (yyyy-mm-dd): _____

注:未满18周岁的未成年人须由父母或监护人代签。Note: The parent or guardian shall sign on behalf of a minor under 18 years old.

五、他人代填申请表时填写以下内容 Part 5: If the application form is completed by another person on the applicant's behalf, please fill out the information of the one who completes the form

5.1 姓名 Name		5.2 与申请人关系 Relationship with the applicant	
5.3 地址 Address		5.4 电话 Phone number	
5.5 声明 Declaration 我声明本人是根据申请人要求而协助填表,证明申请人理解并确认表中所填写内容准确无误。 I declare that I have assisted in the completion of this form at the request of the applicant and that the applicant understands and agrees that the information provided is true and correct.			
代填人签名/Signature: _____ 日期/Date (yyyy-mm-dd): _____			

(资料来源:中国领事服务网,http://cs.mfa.gov.cn/zlbg/bgzl/lhqz/t1066626.shtml。)

Sample 2

外国人签证证件申请表
VISA/ STAY PERMIT / RESIDENCE PERMIT APPLICATION FORM

（请用黑色墨水笔填写内容）

Please complete the form in black ink

近期两寸正面免冠彩色白底照片
3.5 cm×5.3 cm full face recent photo with white background

1. 姓　　　　　　　名　　　　　　　　中文姓名

Surname _____ **Given name** _____ **Name in Chinese** _____

国籍　　　　出生日期　　年　月　日　　出生地

Nationality _____ **Date of birth** _____ Y ___ M ___ D **Place of birth** _____

性别：男　　　女　　电子邮件地址

Sex　M. ☐　　F. ☐　**E-mail** _____

在华单位　　　　　　　　　　　　　　电话：

Company/School in China _____ **Phone No.** _____

在华住址

Address in China _____

境外住址

Overseas address _____

2. 护照种类　　外交　　　　公务（官员）　　　普通　　　　其他

Passport type　Diplomatic ☐　Service (Official) ☐　Ordinary ☐　Other ☐

护照号码　　　　　　　　　有效期至　　　年　　　月　　　日

Passport No. _____ **Valid until** _____ Y ___ M ___ D

3. 现持有效签证证件种类　　签证　　停留证件　　居留证件　　　免签

其他

Current visa category　　Visa☐　　Stay permit☐　　Residence permit☐　　Visa free☐
Others☐

证件号码　　　　　　　　　　　　　　有效期至　　　年　　　　月　　　　日
Visa No. _____　**Valid until** _____ Y _____ M _____ D

4. 使用同一护照的偕行人　Dependents on samepassport

| 姓 | 名 | 性别 | 出生日期 | 与申请人关系 |
| Surname | Given name | Sex | Date of birth | Relationship |

5. 申请签证填写　For visa only

F 访问　　　　　　　L 旅游　　　　　　M 贸易　　　　　Q2 团聚　　　　　J2 记者
Non-commercial business☐　　Tourist☐　　Business☐　　Family reunion☐
Journalist☐

S2 私人事务　　　　　X2 学习　　　　R 人才　　　　　G 过境　　　　　C 乘务
Personal affair☐　　　Student☐　　　Talent☐　　　　Transit☐　　　　Crew☐

团体签证分离　　　　　　　　　　　　团签
Separation from group visa☐　　　Group visa☐

延期　　　　　　换发　　　　　补发　　　　申请本次停留至　　　年　　　月　　　日
Extend☐　　　　Renew☐　　　Reissue☐　　Valid until _____ Y _____ M _____ D

入境次数　　　　停留天数　　　　　　　　入境有效期至　　　　年　　　　月　　　　日
Entries _____ Duration of stay _____ Entry before _____ Y _____ M _____ D

请填写双面　**Please fill out both sides**

6. 申请停留证件填写　For stay permit only

免签	船员	退籍	人道主义	其他
Visa free☐	Crew☐	Renouncement☐	Humanitarian☐	Others☐

换发	补发	申请停留期限至	年	月	日
Renew☐	Reissue☐	Valid until _____	Y _____	M _____	D

7. 申请居留证件填写　For residence permit only

工作	学习	记者	团聚	私人事务
Employee☐	Student☐	Journalist☐	Family reunion☐	Personal affair☐

延期	换发	补发	申请居留期限至	年	月	日
Extend☐	Renew☐	Reissue☐	Valid until _____	Y _____	M _____	D

8. 申请其他证件填写　For other documents

外国人旅行证　　　　　　　　　　　旅行目的地

Foreign citizen travel documents☐　　Destination _____

外国人出入境证　　　　　　　　　　申请日期至　　年　　月　　日

Foreign citizen exit-entry permit☐　　Valid until _____ Y _____ M _____ D

勤工助学或校外实习加注　　　　　　申请日期至　　年　　月　　日

Study-work / Internship☐　　　　　　Valid until _____ Y _____ M _____ D

9. 申请变更填写　For change of the following

姓名	护照号码	事由	增/减偕行人数
Name ☐	Passport No. ☐	Purpose of stay ☐	Add/Reduce number of dependents☐

其他注明

Or others _____

10. 备注 Notes _____

　　我保证以上填写的内容真实、准确、完整，并保证在停留居留期间遵守中华人民共和国的法律。

I hereby declare that the information given above is true, correct and complete. I shall abide by the Chinese laws and regulations during my stay in the People's Republic of China.

申请人签字　　　　　　　　　　　　代办人签字

Applicant's signature _____　　Authorized person's signature _____

手机号码　　　　　　　　　　　　　手机号码

Applicant's Mobile phone No. ____　Authorized person's Mobile phone No. ____

申请日期　　　年　　月　　日　　身份证号码

Application date ___Y ___M ___D　ID card No. _____

单位印章　　　　　　　　　　　　　在京住址

Company/School's seal　　　　　　Address in Beijing _____

（资料来源：北京市公安局，http://gaj.beijing.gov.cn/wsgs/bsbg/crj/202003/t20200331_1763390.html。）

Ⅲ. Useful Words and Expressions

surname n. 姓

given name 名

previous name 曾用名

place of birth 出生地

occupation n. 职业

passport n. 护照

certificate n. 证件

current visa 现持签证

issued by 由(某机关)签发

validity n. 有效期

residence n. 居住,居留

modification n. 变更

accommodation n. 住宿

registration n. 登记,注册

departure n. 离开

seal n. 印章

standard room 标准客房

deluxe room 豪华客房

king size bed 特大床

twin bed (成对的)单人床

Ⅳ. Sentence Examples

1. Have you ever applied for a Chinese visa before? 您是否申请过赴中国签证?

2. Have you ever been declined for your Chinese visa application? 您的赴中国签证申请是否被拒绝过?

3. If ever declined, when and where? 什么时候、在哪被拒的?

4. I hereby declare that the information given above is true, correct and complete. I shall bear the responsibility for the above information.

我谨声明我已如实和完整地填写了上述内容,并对此负责。

5. The room rate is subject to 10% service charge and 3% government tax per room per night.

每个房间每晚要加收 10% 的服务费和 3% 的政府税。

Ⅴ. Notes

1. number of entries requested 拟入境次数

2. intended date of entry 拟入境日期

3. contact in emergency 紧急情况下的联系人

4. local call 本地通话

5. direct access call 直拨电话

6. local fax service 本地传真服务

7. in-room broadband Internet access 室内宽带互联网接入

8. laundry service 洗衣服务

9. business centre 商务中心

Ⅵ. Practice

1. Translation.

①曾用名;②标准客房;③护照的有效期;④申请赴中国签证;⑤current visa;⑥issued by;⑦local call;⑧in-room Internet access.

2. Suppose that you are a foreigner and you are going to visit China. Please fill the Visa or Residence Permit Application Form according to the directions.

Chapter 6

CVs and Cover Letters

Ⅰ. Introductions

You will graduate from a college next year and you are going on a journey of job hunting. When you start this journey, the first things you need are a CV, a cover letter and a self-introduction.

• A CV (curriculum vitae) is a personal summary of your professional history and qualifications for the recruiter to know about you.

• A cover letter is a letter you send to a recruiter alongside your CV.

• And a self-introduction is one of the first things to say when you talk to a recruiter.

Before writing these materials, you should ask yourself several questions.

• First, what is your career goal?

• Second, what are skills and attributes that you would like to highlight? Or, what makes you stand out when competing with others in job hunting?

• Third, what does a recruiter want from a CV, a cover letter or a self-introduction?

Please write the answers in the following forms.

Career goal

The job/post you are interested in or you are planning to do

Skills and other strength you would like to highlight

Skills and strength	Supporting details

* Supporting details are essential to convince the recruiter that you are suitable for the position.

Chapter 6
CVs and Cover Letters

What does a recruiter want from a CV, a cover letter or a self-introduction?

The job/ post you are interested in	The corresponding requirements

Now let's start with writing a CV.

After considering those three questions, you will be aware of what to write in a CV. Knowing your career goal, you can prepare a relevant and targeted application. And you will enrich your CV with an objective understanding of the skills and qualities that you can highlight. Always keep in mind that you should view your CV from a recruiter's perspective.

Below are two sample CVs. Please read them carefully with the following questions in mind:

(1) If you are a recruiter, which one do you prefer at first sight and why?

(2) How does the writer in each CV manage to impress the recruiter, to persuade the recuiter hire them, rather than others?

(3) What is the essential information or details to include in a CV?

(4) Is there any order to follow when introducing details of education or work experiences?

Ⅱ. Sample Reading

Sample 1

Basic Information

Xuanxuan Yang | Female | 22 years old | Shanghai

Mobile：137×××××××× | E-mail：yangxuanxuan@hotmail.com

Education Background

The University of Warwick

2013.9-2014.9 | Industrial Relations and Human Resource Management | Master's Degree

Shanghai University

2009.9-2013.6 | International Politics | Bachelor's Degree

2009.9-2013.6 | English Language and Literature | Bachelor's Degree (Second Degree)

Internship Experience

2013.4-2013.6 | **Korn/Ferry International** | **Research Assistant Intern**

Responsibilities：Conducted executive searching, industry study, company mapping for Luxury team.

2013.3-2013.4 | **McKinsey & Company** | **PTA (Project Intern)**

Responsibilities：Supported Industrial sourcing team for information gathering and cold call.

2012.6-2012.11 | **Glaxo Smith Kline China Investment Ltd.** | **Recruiting Intern**

Responsibilities：Supported daily recruitment tasks for whole team; on-boarding preparation.

Project: Supported "GSK Rx Expansion Project" for two RPO programs (nearlly 100 headcounts in Sales Department).

2012. 4-2012. 5 | TNS Research International | PTA (Project Intern)

Responsibilities: Focused on consumer insight; supported data processing and analysis; conducted case studies; fulfilled report amendment; edited electronic journal "TRU View".

Project: Supported "TRU (Teens Research Unlimited) 2012" (A China teen-and-twenty-something study on their behaviors and attitudes).

2012. 1-2012. 3 | Allianz China Life Insurance Company Ltd. | Staffing Intern

Responsibilities: Supported HR Head and HR staffing team for daily work; supported daily and campus recruitment; employee on-boarding preparation; assisted intern management.

Project: Supported "2012 Allianz China MT Program".

Other Experience

Director of Academic Department, Student Union;

Volunteer of China Human Capital Forum 2011; Volunteer of 2010 Shanghai World Expo.

Honors and Awards

Honored "SHU Excellent Student Leader"; Awarded "SHU General Scholarship" for seven times.

Certificates

IELTS:7. 0 | TEM4 & TEM8 & CET6 (610 points)

Other: Occupational Qualification Certificate of Human Resource Management (Third Level).

Sample 2

He Huihui

(+86) 139×××××××

E-mail:hehuihui@foxmail.com

Education Experience

2019.9-Present	**Shanghai Institute of Tourism**	Tourism English

The Student Work

2019.9-Present   **Shanghai Institute of Tourism**   Commissary in charge of studies

- Assist teachers in their work, collect and sort out homework of each subject.
- Establish communication between students and teachers, and answer students' academic questions when necessary.

2019.9-2020.9   **Publicity Department of Shanghai Institute of Tourism**   Secretary

- Hosted the design work of more than 10 competitions such as the school welcome party and host competition.
- When there was a vacancy in the photography group of the publicity department, I took the initiative to apply for a replacement and successfully completed the photography work.

2020.9-Present   **New Media Club of Shanghai Institute of tourism**   Member

- Run the WeChat public account platform with more than 10000 followers;
- Produced tweets, wrote articles, took photos and edited

videos, with over 500000 views.

Social Experiences

2020.11　　　　**The 3rd China International Import Expo**

- Participated in voluntary activities on behalf of the school as a young volunteer, and provided foreign language translation assistance to Qingpu Public Security Bureau.
- During the volunteer service, I recorded the process of volunteer service with the skills of making videos. The videos were successively published on Jiefang Daily and the official Weibo account of "Youth Shanghai", attracting over 1 million viewers.

2019.10　　　　**The 15th World Wushu Championship**

- Participated in voluntary activities on behalf of the school as a young volunteer, memorized the venue route, did site guidance, and served more than 2000 people.
- Being able to communicate fluently with foreigners, I was temporarily transferred to the translation group to receive foreign guests.

Internship

2019.6-2019.9　　**Guangjie Advertising Company　　Staff**

- Receive customers, answer their needs on the cover design, sort out and summarize to senior designers;
- Handle the company's daily design orders and independently complete simple but large number of designs;
- Participate in the company's advertising projects, providing creative solutions for customers.

Awards

2019-2020	First prize in the Red Tour Guide Competition in Shanghai Institute of Tourism
2019-2020	Shanghai Institute of Tourism's Scholarship for Outstanding Students
2019-2020	Second Prize in the 10th National College Students Red Tourism Creative Planning Competition

Personal Skills

- English   CET 6
- Computer   Proficient in Office suite and multimedia software

Sample 3   Cover letter

Dear sir and madam,

I am responding to your advertisement, for the position of a member of your international business executive team, as it offers the career challenge I am seeking for.

As you will see from my enclosed resume, I am a third-year graduate student from Shanghai Jiaotong University, majoring in preventive medicine. Following are some of my qualities that I would like to highlight.

Observation ability, Logical thinking, Analytical capacity

Starting with a keen interest in reptile pets, I have discovered potential business opportunities in this field. After investigation into the market and analysis of breeds, I decided to invest in several highly profitable varieties of pet lizards, which finally brought me a profit ten times as much as the cost. Meanwhile, the market was always under my observation and analysis. Two years after the beginning, I made a hard and timely decision to quit the business so that I successfully avoided market crash.

Leadership, Team spirit, Interpersonal skills

As the president of the Student Union, I have gained great pleasure to serve students. By leading and organizing various campus activities, I have learned that team work is much more than mutual understanding, and criticism is part of the price of leadership. Coordination and collaboration requires convincing and persuading others in a pleasant way, as well as care and love for the whole team.

Adventurous, Passionate, Resistant to pressure

I took a risk and started my pet business with a loan from the bank. Luckily, my passion and love for reptile pets has been rewarded.

But it was very difficult to take a balance between scientific study, student work and pet business. I was confronted with enormous pressure and fierce challenge from all sides, which in turn offers me enjoyment and meaning of life. The price was that I could only sleep for about 5 hours per day. In this way, I managed to get through the pressure. It was at that time that I realized that I enjoyed challenges and adventures very much.

I have a real enthusiasm in industry analyst, and I believe I am smart and dependable enough to be a match for your requirements.

I am looking forward to your reply and many thanks for your attention.

Yours sincerely,

Li Hua

Now please write down answers to the four questions:

a. If you are a recruiter, which one do you prefer at first sight and why?

b. How does the writer in each CV manage to impress the recruiter, to persuade the recruiter to hire them, rather than others?

c. What is the essential information or details to include in a CV?

1	
2	
3	
4	
5	
...	

d. Is there any order to follow when introducing details of education or work experiences?

For Question a, it's likely that most of us would prefer Sample 2 at the first sight since it looks more organized and clearer. It would be easy to spot the information the recruiters need in Sample 2, while in Sample 1, all the information seems to be piled up with little highlighting.

For Question b, both writers have described their education background, internship experience, and have listed their honors and skills to try to impress the recruiter. In

Sample 2, the information is presented much more in detail than that of Sample 1.

And for Question c, below is the conclusion of what to include in a CV:

- Full name
- Optional information:
  - Date of birth
  - Place of birth
  - Nationality
  - Marital status
- Contact information:
  - Telephone number
  - E-mail address
  - Correspondence address
- Education background
  - Schools or colleges attended
  - Majors and degrees
  - Courses attended (if necessary)
- Work/ internship experience
- Scholarships, honors and awards
- Skills and qualifications

Apart from these major components, there may be other things to include if necessary, such as interests and activities in which achievements were made and a **QR code** as an access to your Wechat account, personal website or vlogs if you would like to show something in new media.

For Question d, there must be an order to follow when presenting education and work experiences. Both Sample 1 and Sample 2 describe these experiences in **reverse chronological order**. If you have a no gaps in your employment history and have not changed jobs too often, you will find reverse chronological order satisfying for such fact-based CVs.

Ⅲ. Useful Words and Expressions

1. I feel greatly honored to apply to your company for a post of junior management trainee.

我感到无比荣幸能申请贵公司管理实习生一职。

2. An advertisement dated on March 3 in *Xinmin Evening*.

刊登在三月三日《新民晚报》上的广告。

3. I am an energetic individual with both practical experience and formal training in hotel/restaurant management.

我精力充沛,拥有实践经验并接受过正规的酒店管理专业培训。

4. I'm sure I shall be qualified for this post.

我确信能胜任该岗位。

5. For the past two years I have worked as part-time clerk.

过去两年我一直做兼职员工。

6. Resort Complex

度假综合区

7. the supervisory, organizational, and communication skills

管理、组织和沟通技能

8. enable me to function successfully as a trainee at one of your resort centers

使我能够胜任贵公司度假中心实习生一职

9. In June I will be receiving an associate's degree in hotel management from Zhongshan University.

六月我将获得中山大学酒店管理大专学历。

10. to work harmoniously with others

与同事工作相处和谐

11. Complementing my work experience and studies are personal qualities that will make me a successful manager.

除了工作经历与学业成绩,我的个性特点也会有助于我成为一名成功的经理人。

12. at a time convenient for you

在您方便的时候

13. major in Tourism Management with emphasis in Travel Agency

旅游管理专业旅行社方向

14. Excellent Student

优秀学生或三好学生

15. community services and other social interactive work

社区服务和其他社交工作

IV. Sentence Examples

1. I'd like to apply to your company for a post of junior management trainee.

我想向贵公司申请管理实习生一职。

2. I shall take responsibility for those decisions.

我将对这些决定负责。

3. I would appreciate the opportunity to discuss my qualifications.

能有机会和您探讨我的申请资格,我觉得很荣幸。

4. I enjoy serving customers and meeting challenges the public service demands.

我喜欢为客人服务并喜欢迎接挑战。

V. Notes

1. Date of Birth 出生日期,可缩写为 DOB
2. M. A. 为硕士学位,B. A. 为学士学位,Doctor's degree 为博士学位
3. references 这里指推荐信或推荐人

VI. Practice

1. Translation.

①我相信我的经验和推荐人可以证明,我符合贵公司计调一职的特定需要。

②Since leaving school, I have attended Typewriting and Shorthand classes, and have now attained a speed of fifty and ninety words respectively.

2. We all know that Tu Youyou was awarded the Nobel Prize in Physiology or Medicine in 2015. Please search Tu Youyou online and then write a resume for her.

3. Write a cover letter for a post of an assistant manager to a travel agency in Shanghai.

4. Would you please design your own resume?

Chapter 7

Contracts in Tourism Industry

Ⅰ. Introductions

Tourism contracts, including tourism agreements, are legal texts. They are clauses related to rights and obligations of both parties signed in accordance with the law, and are legally binding on parties. With the rapid development of the tourism industry and the increase in foreign business exchanges, signing various contracts in the tourism industry has become an important means for various sectors of the tourism industry to communicate with foreign businesses, ensure the rights and obligations of both parties, and ensure cooperation.

Tourism contracts include the following types: cooperation contracts, reservation contracts, sales contracts, employment contracts, lease contracts, and commission contracts. A contract is generally composed of the following parts: the title of the contract, main clauses, the conclusion, and signatures of both parties. Some contracts may contain additional clauses.

When signing a contract, please pay attention to the following points:

Clarity of information

Contracts often involve the quantity of transactions and the quality of products. In order to avoid unnecessary disputes, the quantity and measurement unit should be specified, such as the number and price of hotel rooms, the number and price of various types of tickets, etc.

The formality of language

Since contracts are legal texts, the language of contracts does not allow any ambiguity or misunderstanding. Therefore, in English contracts, passive voice, compound clauses and archaic words are often avoided to use.

Ⅱ. Sample Reading

Sample 1　中外旅行社合作合同范本

Model Contract on Tours Arranged by Chinese and Foreign Travel Services

China _____ International Travel Service (hereinafter referred to as Party A) and _____ (hereinafter referred to as Party B) have, on the basis of equality, mutual benefit and friendly cooperation, reached the following agreement and signed this contract on mutual rights and obligations in the development of the joint industry.

The contract and the appendix to the contract constitute an inseparable integrity. Both the transcript of the contract and the articles in the appendix to the contract hold the same authenticity.

Article 1

Party B plans _____ to organize _____ tours (or delegations) with

tourists to visit China from _____ to _____.

Article 2

Party B is required to confirm to Party A the final booking on a tour (or a delegation), whenever accepted by Party A, 30 days prior to the scheduled arrival of the said tour (or delegation) at the point of entry in China.

Party A should acknowledge confirmation to Party B within three working days after receipt of confirmation from Party B.

Party B is required to send Party A, at least 20 days prior to the scheduled arrival of each tour (or delegation) at the point of entry in China, a detailed list with each participant's full name, sex, date of birth, occupation, nationality, passport number, arrival/departure flight or train number, points and dates of entry and exit, number of rooms required and requests on visits.

Article 3

Party B is free to propose at any time to Party A additional tours (or delegations) other than those planned. Upon receipt of mail/fax/E-mail proposal from Party B, Party A is required to reply within three working days. Upon receipt of a reply from Party A, Party B is required to acknowledge confirmation to Party A also within three working days, with necessary information as required by Article 2.

Article 4

Party B agrees to make telegraphic remittance of total expenses for each tour (or delegation) to Party A's bankaccount at least 15 days prior to the scheduled arrival in China of each tour (or delegation). If more than one remittance is made simultaneously, it is necessary for Party B to specify the exact amount for each tour (or delegation) on the remittance memo. Tour expenses are not to be settled in Chinese currency RMB.

Article 5

If Party B fails to make the remittance before the deadline as stipulated by Article 4, Party A has the right to take any of the three following options to deal with the overdue payment:

(1) Party A will not host the tour (or delegation) any longer, no matter whether the tour (or delegation) has entered into China or not. Party B will bear all responsibilities arising therefrom.

(2) Party A will report the case to the travel administration of the Chinese government and propose to all other travel services in China declining hospitality to the unpaid tour (or delegation) sent by Party B.

(3) Party A will charge Party B an overdue fine for any unpaid amount. After the conclusion of each tour (or delegation) in China, Party B is required to clear off any outstanding amount within one month, otherwise an overdue fine is to be charged additionally in the following month, at a rate of 0.2% of the outstanding amount per day.

Article 6

Party A is committed to offer services according to the itineraries and package services confirmed by this contract and the appendix to the contract.

Party A has the obligation to instruct all its liaison personnel, tourguide, drivers and other staff to render standard-oriented services to tourists. They are strictly forbidden to extort tipping from tourists.

Article 7

Except in situations beyond human control, Party A should provide compensatory service for tourists or refund to Party B the difference in payment for service rendered below standard.

Except in situations beyond human control, Party A will be held responsible for any additional expenses resulting from the change, caused by Party A, in itinerary, transportation vehicles, accommodation and meals.

However, Party A will not be held responsible for compensation resulting from change of itinerary under the following situations:

(1) The scheduled date of entry of a tour (or delegation) is changed off hand by

Party B.

Consequently Party B will be liable for compensation and complaints lodged by clients, resulting from change of accommodation, transportation and sightseeing program. Party B is also liable for economic loss, if any, incurred to Party A.

(2) The itinerary is changed at the request of tour (or delegation) participants after arrival in China.

Subsequent economic loss, if any, will be borne by tour (or delegation) participants rather than Party A.

(3) The tour schedule, itinerary and days of stay in China are changed due to unforeseen situation beyond human control. Any difference or balance in payment will be collected or reimbursed accordingly.

(4) Party A will not be held responsible for any harm sustained by tourists during their visit in China by airplane/trains or steamship or during their stay in hotel, restaurant or tourist area.

However, Party A is obligated to help Party B to reduce the harm in humanitarian spirit.

Article 8

Party B reserves the right to lodge complaint to the travel administration of the Chinese government and moreover to request compensation for material loss, as a result of violation by Party A of provisions for quality service.

Article 9

Party A should notify Party B, 30 days in advance of the scheduled arrival of a tour (or delegation) in China, the adjustment, if needed under unusual circumstance, in the package rates after confirmed by both parties. Party A will charge the tour (or delegation) based on original quotation within three months after the date of notification.

Article 10

It is necessary for Party A to make Party B acquainted with the policy and regulations of the Chinese government concerning tourist activities in China. Party B is required to ask tourists to abide with the policy and regulations. Party A will not be held responsible for any violation by tourists against the Chinese policy and regulations, which will be dealt with by law in China.

Article 11

Party A will quote a package rate for a tour (or delegation) scheduled to China according to Chinese pricing policy and regulation. After the quotation is confirmed by Party B, both parties will sign an appendix to the contract. There is (are) appendix (appendices) attached to this contract.

Article 12

Party A is committed to making overall arrangements as various cities in China for tours (delegations) sponsored by Party B. Party A can not entrust any other Party to become involved in separate arrangements for tours (delegations) at any city in China. Party A can entrust, if necessary, a certified land operator in China to take care of travel arrangements. As an immediate agent for Party B, Party A will bear direct responsibility for tourist activities in China.

Article 13

To guarantee security for travel in China, Party A will arrange for tourists' travel-accident-insurance, which will be covered in tour package rates. Either party is liable for violation, if any, against regulations stipulated by the Chinese government concerning insurance coverage for overseas tourists during travel in China.

Article 14

The conclusion, alternation and abrogation of this contract or retrieval of breach of contract should be in line with the regulations specified in the "People's Republic of China Law Concerning Economic Contract with Foreign Countries". Without mutual consent, either party cannot transfer, to a third Party, its right and commitments, as described in this contract.

Article 15

Both Parties should try to resolve, through friendly consultation, their disputes, if any, in the execution of the contract. If no solution could be found through consultation, both parties agree to submit their disputes to China National Tourism Administration for coordinated settlement in accordance with the law of China.

Article 16

This contract will be effective, once signed by both parties, and valid until _____. After expiration, the validity of the contract can be extended, under a written agreement confirmed by both parities.

Article 17

This contract is written in Chinese and English. Both versions have the same authenticity. Whenever difference in explanation arises between the two versions, the Chinese version will be regarded as the criterion of judgment.

Article 18

After both parties have signed this contract, Party A should submit a duplicate copy of the contract to its superior tourism authorities for record.

Sample 2　团体游客订房协议

Reservation Agreement

Huating Hotel (hereinafter to be called as the first party) and Cook Travel (hereinafter to be called as the second party) have reached an agreement on room reservation for tour groups as follows:

Period

The first party agrees to bring into effect the hotel reservation of 26 tour groups from the second party in 2010.

Room Rates

Room rate for a double room per night is 350 yuan (RMB).

Room Reservation

(1) The second party should provide the first party with the number of groups, number of total persons, the amount of rooms requested, the arrival and departure date of the groups by January 2010.

(2) The second party should give the first party a general confirmation for next month's groups. The confirmation includes:

①tour code of the group;

②date of arrival and departure and means of transportation;

③number of persons and number of rooms needed.

Account settlement

(1) The second party should remit 10000 yuan as a deposit to the first party while making reservation. The first party will not guarantee the rooms requested without receiving the **remittance**.

(2) The second party should remit the full amount of hotel rental cost and meal expenses to the first party's account 30 days prior to the arrival of each group.

Modification and Cancellation

(1) No cancellation fee will be charged when the first party is informed 20 days prior to the arrival of the group. Room cost of the whole group of a day will be charged if cancellation is received within 20 days prior to the arrival of the group.

(2) It is mutually agreed that both sides should bear 50% of a day's room charge as financial losses of delay due to transportation.

Other

(1) Both sides should act according to this agreement. Should there be any violation by the second party against any of the stipulation in this agreement, or should

there be a transfer of any rights, without the consent of the first party, the first party has the right to cancel this agreement.

(2) This agreement is valid from January 1, 2010 to December. 31, 2010 and effective from the date of the signing of both sides.

Huating Hotel	Cook Travel
by	by
General Manager	General Manager
Date: Oct. 26, 2009	Date: Oct. 26, 2009

Ⅲ. Useful Words and Expressions

hereinafter adv. 此后

appendix n. 附属条款

authenticity n. 真实性

remittance n. 汇款

liaison n. 联络

quotation n. 报价

abrogation n. 取消

expiration n. 过期

confirmation n. 确认

retrieval n. 挽回

breach n. 违反

extort v. 敲诈勒索

violation n. 违反

cancellation n. 取消

Ⅳ. Sentence Examples

1. All disputes arising from the execution of or in connection with the contract shall be settled through friendly consultation between both parties. In case no settlement can be reached, the dispute shall be submitted for arbitration.

凡因执行合同或与合同有关事项所发生的争端,应由双方通过友好协商加以解决。如未能达成协议,则应付诸仲裁。

2. Any dispute arising out of this contract shall be settled through friendly negotiation.

执行合同中产生的争端应通过友好协商加以解决。

3. The present contract is made out in Chinese and English, both versions being equally valid.

本合同用中文和英文两种文字写成,两个版本具有同等效力。

4. Neither party shall cancel the contract without sufficient cause or reason.

双方均不得无故解除合同。

5. We are entitled to cancel the contract which became overdue owing to buyer's no-performance.

我们有权取消由于买方不能履行而延误的合同。

6. Should any other clause in this contract be in conflict with the following supplementary conditions, the supplementary conditions should be taken as final and binding.

如本合同的其他任何条款与附加条款有冲突,以本附加条款为准。

7. If one side fails to observe the contract, the other side is entitled to cancel it.

如果一方不信守合同,另一方有权终止合同。

8. China International Travel Service(hereinafter referred to as A) and the Ocean Hotel (hereinafter referred to as B) desirous to strengthen the friendly relations between the two parties on the basis of equality and for their mutual benefit, have agreed to conclude this agreement as follows.

中国国际旅行社(以下简称A方)与远洋宾馆(以下简称B方)为了加强双方友好关系,在平等互利的基础上,愿意达成以下协议。

9. Wishing to promote tourism and to expand cooperation of two parties, A and B have agreed as follows.

为了促进旅游业发展及拓展合作,甲乙双方达成以下协议。

Ⅴ. Notes

1. sale contract 销售合同
2. purchase contract 买卖合同
3. booking contract 预订合同
4. Party A 甲方
5. Party B 乙方
6. travel-accident-insurance 旅游意外保险
7. overdue payment 逾期罚款
8. land operator 地接社
9. bring into effect 生效
10. account settlement 结账

Ⅵ. Practice

1. Translation.

①合同自签订之日起生效。

②双方就订房一事达成协议。

③任何预定从确认书收到之时起生效。

④你方将得到5%的佣金。

⑤A 10% commission will be paid each individual guest room.

⑥The hotel will provide one complementary bed for every 15 paying guests in tour.

⑦Meal arrangements, meeting and receptions should be requested at the earliest possible convenience to reserve the function rooms.

2. Write a contract of room reservation for independent travelers.

Chapter 8

Advertisements in Tourism Industry

Ⅰ. Introductions

Travel advertising is a form of publicity. The purpose of advertising is to provide information, promote demand, and promote sales. The purpose of tourism advertising is to attract the attention of potential tourists, arouse the interest of tourists, provide them with rich tourism information, and ultimately arouse their desire to consume.

Tourism is a comprehensive industry. The six elements of tourism (food, accommodation, transportation, travelling, shopping, and entertainment) determine the diversity of the tourism sector, such as transportation, travel agencies, hotels, restaurants, and entertainment activities. The services provided by various industries are different, so their advertisements should also have their own characteristics, but components of these advertisements should be similar: company name, description (introducing the content, features, precautions of the service or product), illustrations (optional, in order to stimulate the senses of potential visitors, resulting in consuming behavior), corporate address and contact information, etc.

In order to achieve the purpose of advertising, the following points should be noted when writing tourism advertisements:

Highlight characteristics

Different tourists have different needs. Characteristics should be highlighted in order to meet the needs of tourists and increase the attractiveness of advertising.

Authenticity

Tourism advertising must insist on authenticity and not be too exaggerated. Tourism products and services should be introduced in order to win the trust of customers.

Conciseness

Advertisements should be short and eye-catching. The language of the advertisements should be concise and convincing. Avoid using complex and difficult sentences in advertising language, and generally use imperative sentences to arouse tourists' desire to buy.

Ⅱ. Sample Reading

Sample 1 Beijing Daxing International Airport, China

Never one to do things by halves, China is building a huge (and much-needed) second international gateway for Beijing. A 780000 square meter terminal designed by Zaha Hadid is set to open in September in the south of the capital, and plans to serve 72 million passengers a year. When fully operational, the Centre for Aviation says that figure could rise to 100 million. The existing Beijing Capital International Airport was the world's second busiest airport by passenger volume in 2017, seeing 95.8 million passengers. Meanwhile the Civil Aviation Administration of China says the country

aims to add 216 new airports by the year 2035, while developing regional hubs.

Sample 2　Advertisement of travel agencies

When your clients ask for the moon...

Offer them paradise with WALKERS TOURS

Tempt them with Sri Lanka...

...pure tropic strands, exciting ancient cities, enchanting scenery and exotic wild life, fragrant spice and tea gardens, sapphier and ruby mines and glittering oriental pageants.

Walkers Tours package Dream Holidays in Sri Lanka (perhaps, till Ceylon to you), with skill and flair. We are versatile and diversified—we handle individuals, groups, families, the young and young-at-heart; deluxe incentive tours and ship-to-shore excursions. We understand adventure seekers as well as stayput beach addicts.

Our special interest packages range from Buddhist culture and meditation, gem prospecting, golf and tea gardens, tropical fauna to archaeological excavations and ethic festivals.

And our resources include a chain of distinctive hotels in prime locations and the largest tourist ground-transport fleet.

Walkers Tours Limited.

130 Glennie Street, Colombo 2, Sri Lanka.

Tel: 27540, 548030 548031   Telex: 21228, 21582, 21389,

Cables: "WALKIN" Colombo.

We are No. 1 in Paradise.

Sample 3   Advertisement of travel products

Package Tours

Shanghai-Suzhou-Hangzhou-Xi'an-Beijing

Tour Code: P005

Duration: 11 days/ 10 nights

Arrival on Everyday

Highlights: Your journey starts from Shanghai, China's most modern metropolis. Then visit elegant classic gardens and the Beijing-Hangzhou Grand Canal in Suzhou, cruise on the legendary West Lake and taste the "Dragon Well" Tea in Hangzhou. Continue to Xi'an in Central China to admire the 6000 life-sized Terra-cotta Warriors. The last stop of this memorable trip is "Capital Beijing" to discover its timeless imperial treasures including the Forbidden City and the Great Wall.

Joint Tours

Beijing-Xi'an-Shanghai

Tour Code: BXS

Duration: 10 days/ 9 nights

Arrival on Saturday

Highlights: With 7 UNESCO sites & the big event of Shanghai Expo included;

Programs of Guarantee Departures & Full Packages based on minimum 2 people joint tour & extension available; The real deal for a great value, enriched with more inclusive best-selected sightseeing for the full enjoyable tours.

Special Seasonal Promotion

Shanghai Stopover

Tour Code: SSPS

Duration: 5 days/ 4 nights

Arrival on Friday

Highlights: Special Seasonal Promotion, Unbelievable Lowest Price from November, 2010, to April, 2011; Programs of Guarantee Departures & Full Packages based on minimum 2 people joint tour; Available to the Exclusive Groups.

Sample 4　Advertisement of airline companies

Qatar Airways — Going Places Together

Every moment of your time together is precious. That is why we are dedicated to providing a premium service from the minute you check-in, to the moment you land in any of more than 150 places we fly to worldwide. Together we can create experiences to cherish and memories that last a lifetime.

Qatarairways.com

Singapore Airlines — A Great New Way to Fly

Extra Comfort. Extra Choices. Extra Privileges.

When it comes to flying, there are little things that make the journey great.

Like more comfortable seats, additional meals , beverage choices, and exclusive privileges. All brought together by the same award-winning services you love.

It's just one of lengths we go to, to bring you a great new way to fly.

Sample 5　Advertisements of hotels

Welcome To The Nile Front Cottages

Indulge in blissful greenery edged with breathtaking views and unwind in the soothing breeze of the Nile. Welcome to the incredible experience at Nile front — embark on an unforgettable new journey with us! Wonderful experiences always start here.

Nestled on the banks of the Victoria Nile, Nile Front Cottages offers a unique luxury getaway in pristine wooden cabins overlooking the Nile. Wake up to the sounds of chirping birds and indulge in nature in our leafy compound or enjoy the breeze of the lake from the beautiful stone terrace overlooking the Nile.

Our guests can enjoy a beautiful and quiet escape yet remain close to key tourist sites and top hangouts & eateries within Jinja town, Uganda's first industrial town and home to the source of the Nile. The old Ferry Port, the Jinja Golf & Tennis club and the Source of the Nile are all within a walking distance from our location. While staying with us look out for our pop-up Spin Cycling classes or our open air cinema experience that are free for guests.

W Hotels debuts in Japan

Marriott has debuted its W Hotels brand in Japan, with a new property in Osaka.

The W Osaka is located on the city's Midosuji Boulevard, within a building designed by Osaka-born architect Tadao Ando. The minimalist black monolith façade is designed to conceal the colourful interiors by Amsterdam-based studio Concrete — the creative brains behind the W London and W Verbier in Switzerland.

Marriott describes the design concept as paying homage to the Edo Period, during which "excessive displays of wealth were prohibited, and merchants were said to have dressed modestly in public" but opulently in private.

Upon entering the hotel, guests will be greeted by an illuminated tunnel inspired by the Japanese art forms of origami and kirigami, with images of nature and seasons reflected on the walls.

Additionally, each alternate floor features either pink or blue colour schemes and neon lights to represent Japan's cherry blossoms and Osaka's azure oceanside.

Meanwhile, 337 rooms and suites feature bright spaces, clean lines and bold colour schemes, drawing inspiration from Osaka's streetscape. Rooms include floor-to-ceiling windows with views of the skyline, spacious bathrooms with rain showers and "luxe amenities to retreat and recharge". Within the wardrobes, there is a graphic depicting the city's famous landmarks by pixel art group eBoy.

The hotel also boasts a 27th floor penthouse suite with features including artwork by Dutch textile artist Sigrid Calon, a bathtub designed to resemble a champagne bucket, and a built-in DJ booth which the group states is the "first of its kind in a hotel room in Japan".

Dining venues include French brasserie Oh La La led by Chef Yusuke Takada, Japanese restaurant Teppanyaki MYDO, and omakase—style Sushi UKIYO. There is also a patisserie called Mixup, and a Wet Bar offering cocktails next to the 20-metre indoor pool.

The hotel's third-floor Living Room — W's take on the lobby — features vivid colours and a design of Kawaii Kokeshi wooden dolls. The space will host events such as standup comedy and DJ sets, and serve cocktails and the hotel's own private-label champagne.

Further facilities include a 24-hour fitness centre with a yoga room, an indoor pool with an LED ceiling, and a spa with five treatment rooms, all of which are located on the fourth floor. There are also four event and meeting spaces, including a ballroom.

Rajeev Menon, President, Asia Pacific (excluding China), Marriott International, commented:

"Osaka's mix of culture and bold, high-energy lifestyle makes it the ideal setting for the debut of W Hotels in Japan. We are excited to once again be partnering with Sekisui House to welcome W Osaka to the luxury hospitality landscape here, and know international travelers and locals alike will be drawn to the hotel and its playground of possibilities."

Jennie Toh, Vice President of Brand Marketing and Brand Management, Asia Pacific, Marriott International, added:

"The energy and eclecticism of Japan, particularly Osaka, make it the perfect backdrop for a W hotel. From unforgettable dining experiences and live music sets to the thoughtful design rooted in the history and culture of the city, W Osaka is a destination within a destination where international jetsetters and local tastemakers meet and make magic."

Ⅲ. Useful Words and Expressions

paradise n. 大堂

versatile adj. 多才多艺的，多用途的

incentive n. 奖励

addict n. 入迷者

package n. 包裹，套餐

fleet n. 车队，船队

brochure n. 小册子

metropolis n. 国际大都市

legendary adj. 传奇的

Ⅳ. Sentence Examples

1. Our products are versatile and diversified.

我们的旅游产品丰富多彩。

2. We handle individuals, groups, families, the young and young-at-heart; deluxe incentive tours and ship-to-shore excursions.

我们承接个人旅行、团队旅行、家庭旅行、青年旅游和老年人旅行；豪华奖励旅游以及水上、岸上的短途旅游。

3. Our special interest packages range from Buddhist culture, golf and tea gardens, tropical fauna to archaeological excavations and ethic festivals.

我们的特殊兴趣包团游产品丰富多彩，例如佛教文化之旅、高尔夫和茶园之旅、热带动物之旅、考古发掘之旅、民族节庆旅游。

4. Our resources include a chain of distinctive hotels in prime locations and the largest tourist ground-transport fleet.

我们资源丰富，拥有黄金地段的特色酒店和最大的旅游车队。

5. Our services range from arranging well-planned itineraries for groups/individuals/business executives to issuing travelers cheques, acceptable world wide,

freighting cargo and other allied travel activities.

我们的服务范围广泛,包括为团队、个人和商务人士安排精选的旅游线路,签发旅行支票,可接受全球范围内的货物运输和其他旅游活动。

6. Continue to Xi'an in Central China to admire the 6000 life-sized Terra-cotta Warriors.

接着去中国西安,欣赏6000个栩栩如生的兵马俑。

7. The real deal for a great value, enriched with more inclusive best-selected sightseeing for full enjoyable tours.

该产品物超所值,有全包的精选的观光项目,令您拥有一个圆满愉快的行程。

8. Special Seasonal Promotion, Unbelievable Lowest Price.

特别的季节促销,难以置信的超低价格。

9. Contact Pacific Delight, a leader in travel to China, for our free 56-page color brochure.

联系我们,太平洋喜悦旅游——中国旅游的领先者,索取免费的56页彩色宣传册子。

Ⅴ. Notes

1. incentive tour 奖励旅游
2. special interest tour 特殊兴趣旅游
3. package tour 包价游
4. joint tour 组合游(散客拼团)
5. prime location 黄金地带
6. ground-transport fleet 地面交通团队
7. Beijing-Hangzhou Grand Canal 京杭大运河
8. Terra-cotta Warrior 兵马俑

9. the Forbidden City 紫禁城

10. UNESCO 联合国教科文组织

Ⅵ. Practice

1. Translation.

①我们的业务范围包括飞机票、火车票、轮船票预订和酒店预订。

②我们的酒店位于市中心的黄金地段。

③我航空公司经营二十多条国际和地区的航线、四十条国内航线。

④Location—Exclusive lake front location in the middle of the city.

⑤We are well equipped with seven F&B facilities offering Cantonese, Western and Japanese cuisine; bars and lounges.

⑥We offer all kinds of tours, such as all-inclusive tours, joint tours, independent tours, etc.

⑦Our package includes: 5 nights accommodation with buffet breakfast at Shanghai Galaxy Hotel; Round trip airport-hotel-airport transfers; a half-day tour in Shanghai; tours with meals in Suzhou and Hangzhou.

⑧Our package excludes: optional tours in Shanghai, international flights & airport tax, personal expenses & gratuities to guide, drivers & porters.

2. Please write an advertisement for Jinggang Mountain(井冈山).

[1] 傅似逸. 英语写作:应用文写作[M]. 2版. 北京:北京大学,2015.

[2] 雪莉·泰勒. 商务英语写作实例精解[M]. 7版. 北京:外语教学与研究出版社,2014.

[3] Reid J. Five International Airports Opening in 2019[EB/OL]. (2019-01-05)[2021-07-01]. https://www.businesstraveller.com/business-travel/2019/01/05/five-international-airports-opening-in-2019/.

[4] Poitevien J. Lindt Opens World's Largest Chocolate Museum—With the World's Largest Chocolate Fountain[EB/OL]. (2020-09-12)[2021-07-01]. https://www.travelandleisure.com/food-drink/lindt-home-of-chocolate-zurich-museum-opening.

[5] Maker A. Lounge Review:British Airways Galleries Club Lounge (North), Heathrow Terminal 5[EB/OL]. (2020-04-15)[2021-07-01]. https://www.businesstraveller.com/tried-and-tested/lounge-review-british-airways-galleries-club-lounge-north-heathrow-terminal-5/.

[6] Poitevien J. Ride Through the Great Smoky Mountains During Peak Fall Foliage With This Railroad Experience[EB/OL]. (2020-10-06)[2021-07-01]. https://www.travelandleisure.com/trip-ideas/fall-vacations/great-smoky-mountains-railroad-fall-foliage-ride.

[7] Brandler H. W Hotels Debuts in Japan[EB/OL]. (2021-03-16)[2021-07-01]. https://www.businesstraveller.com/business-travel/2021/03/16/w-hotels-debuts-in-japan/.

教学支持说明

高等院校应用型人才培养"十四五"规划旅游管理类系列教材系华中科技大学出版社"十四五"期间重点教材。

为了改善教学效果,提高教材的使用效率,满足高校授课教师的教学需求,本套教材备有与纸质教材配套的教学课件(PPT电子教案)和拓展资源(案例库、习题库、视频等)。

为保证本教学课件及相关教学资料仅为教材使用者所用,我们将向使用本套教材的高校授课教师免费赠送教学课件或相关教学资料,烦请授课教师通过电话、邮件或加入旅游专家俱乐部QQ群等方式与我们联系,获取"教学课件资源申请表"文档,准确填写后发给我们,我们的联系方式如下:

地址:湖北省武汉市东湖新技术开发区华工科技园华工园六路

邮编:430223

电话:027-81321911

传真:027-81321917

E-mail:lyzjjlb@163.com

旅游专家俱乐部QQ群号:306110199

旅游专家俱乐部QQ群二维码:

群名称:旅游专家俱乐部
群　号:306110199

教学课件资源申请表

填表时间：_____年___月___日

1. 以下内容请教师按实际情况填写，★为必填项。
2. 学生根据个人情况如实填写，相关内容可以酌情调整提交。

★姓名		★性别	□男 □女	出生年月		★职务	
						★职称	□教授 □副教授 □讲师 □助教

★学校		★院/系	
★教研室		★专业	
★办公电话		家庭电话		★移动电话	
★E-mail（请填写清晰）		★QQ号/微信号	
★联系地址		★邮编	

★现在主授课程情况	学生人数	教材所属出版社	教材满意度
课程一			□满意 □一般 □不满意
课程二			□满意 □一般 □不满意
课程三			□满意 □一般 □不满意
其 他			□满意 □一般 □不满意

教 材 出 版 信 息						
方向一		□准备写	□写作中	□已成稿	□已出版待修订	□有讲义
方向二		□准备写	□写作中	□已成稿	□已出版待修订	□有讲义
方向三		□准备写	□写作中	□已成稿	□已出版待修订	□有讲义

请教师认真填写表格下列内容，提供索取课件配套教材的相关信息，我社将根据每位教师/学生填表信息的完整性、授课情况与索取课件的相关性，以及教材使用的情况赠送教材的配套课件及相关教学资源。

ISBN（书号）	书名	作者	索取课件简要说明	学生人数（如选作教材）
			□教学 □参考	
			□教学 □参考	

★您对与课件配套的纸质教材的意见和建议，希望提供哪些配套教学资源：